Political Discourse

L. H. LaRUE

Political Discourse

A CASE STUDY OF THE WATERGATE AFFAIR

The University of Georgia Press

Athens and London

© 1988 by the University of Georgia Press
Athens, Georgia 30602
All rights reserved

Designed by Sandra Strother Hudson
Set in Linotron 10 on 13 Trump Mediaeval

The paper in this book meets the guidelines
for permanence and durability of the Committee on
Production Guidelines for Book Longevity of the
Council on Library Resources.

Printed in the United States of America
92 91 90 89 88   5 4 3 2 1

Library of Congress Cataloging in Publication Data

LaRue, L. H.
  Political discourse.
  Bibliography: p.
  Includes index.
    1. Watergate Affair, 1972–1974.   2. Nixon, Richard M.
(Richard Milhous), 1913–   . Impeachment.
I. Title
E860.L37   1988   364.1'32'0973   87-13279
ISBN 0-8203-0980-X (alk. paper)
ISBN 0-8203-1027-1 (pbk.: alk. paper)

British Library Cataloging in Publication Data available.

FOR SUSAN, ANDREA, AND JAMES

Though for no other cause, yet for this: that posterity
may know we have not loosely through silence
permitted things to pass away as in a dream . . .
———Richard Hooker,
Of the Laws of Ecclesiastical Polity (1593)

CONTENTS

ACKNOWLEDGMENTS

I would like to thank those who have made a special contribution to this book. First, Joseph E. Ulrich and Andrew W. McThenia, Jr.: we began teaching together many years ago, and over the course of our lives as colleagues we have talked for many hours about the relationship between law and life; I know that I have stolen much from these conversations, but I couldn't begin to say what. Second, James Boyd White: in conversation he helped me get started; his own published work was an inspiration; and his skill as a reader was invaluable in suggesting improvements. Third, Jan G. Deutsch and Brian C. Murchison: at those times when I was bogged down, each gave my manuscript a reading that pushed me on toward a better book.

But most important, I would thank my wife, my daughter, and my son, to whom this book is dedicated. In the course of our life together, we have spent countless hours around the dining room table, talking about the things that matter. I dedicate this book to the memory of those conversations.

1   THE QUESTION

As I finish this book, a decade has passed since Richard Nixon resigned and thus gave up the office of the presidency. He did so under pressure, for it seemed clear that he was going to be impeached and then convicted of "high crimes and misdemeanors" (this is the constitutional phrase for an impeachable offense) because of his role in what was called "the Watergate affair." Had he been convicted, he would have been removed from office involuntarily. One can say that he left so that he wouldn't be thrown out.

But what did he do that was so bad? Why was it bad? I shall write about this matter, but I wish to write mainly about something else: What about us? Why did we think that what he did was a "high crime and misdemeanor"? This latter question is important, since our actions in those days, what we said and what we did, say as much about us as they do about Nixon. The general principle behind this assertion—that what we said reveals as much about us as about him—is a simple and obvious one. There are many ways to describe events like Watergate, and of course, this assertion is true of most events. One selects facts, characterizes them, and arranges them, and there are countless ways of selecting and characterizing. Since there are so many ways of describing, it is likely that any particular description will tell us more about the person describing than the event described. So too with Watergate.

In short, my thesis is that the rhetoric of the public debate over Watergate tells us some important things about ourselves, our character, and our aspirations as a people. This debate occurred in many places, from arguments over coffee or beer to arguments in the Capitol Building of the United States. All of this discussion, from the most informal to the most formal, could be examined for clues about what it might reveal of our character and aspirations. No record was left of most of these debates, but our representatives in Congress did leave a public record of their argument. They were our representatives, and so I would like to examine what they represented us to be. Those who serve in Congress are experts in many things, but one feature of their expertise is that they are knowledgeable about what can safely be said in public. Members of Congress who say things that are not publicly acceptable will soon be voted out. Consequently, I think that we should pay especial attention to what they did say. In offering their arguments about Watergate, they made judgments about the types of rhetoric that were publicly acceptable. In doing so, they made judgments about who we are. I wish to ask whether they portrayed us as we would wish to be portrayed.

As one examines our representatives' arguments, it becomes apparent that they disagreed about many of the most important sorts of things. Their rhetoric does not reveal a uniform harmony. There are inconsistencies, contradictions, and conflict. My thesis shall be that the most fundamental conflict was over the choice between two metaphors, the metaphor of "the rule of law" and the metaphor of "a breach of trust." I wish to present in this book the way in which these two metaphors were used, the way in which they could lead to different sorts of judgments, and the importance of the difference.

My own judgment is that the rhetoric which prevailed, the primary rhetoric that was employed, was the rhetoric centered in the metaphor of the rule of law. In many ways the rhetoric was admirable, but I also think that this way of talking about Watergate and the impeachment of the president failed in expressing what was at stake. To the extent that our representatives limited themselves to talk about the rule of law, they failed us. I do not wish to suggest that what they said was wrong, or misplaced, but I do wish to argue that it was seriously incomplete. My own judgment is that the metaphor of breach of trust would have been better: less legalistic, more inclusive, more reflective of the ethical issues that were at stake. In using the metaphor of the rule of law, our representatives did express some of our cultural expectations and aspirations; even so, they could have expressed more. Had they made the metaphor of a breach of trust their primary one, they would have been able to incorporate more of our hopes; they would have represented us better.

However, my judgment about what we should say is a conclusion, not a beginning, and it belongs at the end of the book. I put it up front so that readers may know where I am heading—forewarned is forearmed—but now I must make a proper beginning. I shall do so by justifying my enterprise, and my justification begins with one of the most interesting "facts" about the Watergate affair: in the eyes of the world, what we did was strange. Conversations with people who are citizens of another country quickly show that those whose culture differs from ours were astonished that we would drive a president from office because of what had happened; in their judgment, what happened was trivial. We differ from the world, and yet despite this difference, none of the books on Watergate try to explain what is different about us. The fault I find with most books on Watergate is that they are written on the assumption that Nixon and his associates are the only ones who are strange, so that the only thing that needs to be explained is them. I would like to start with the assumption that we too need to be explained. Of course, we can pretend that our response was "natural" and that any "rational" person would respond as we did. But this claim would be absurd. Rational people in other nations did not "naturally" respond to the revelations about Nixon as we did. Consequently, I am confident that we need to know more about who we are, about what sort of people we are, and about how different we are.

An inquiry into what we did and who we are is hard to make, and one of the difficulties is that it is hard to avoid self-deception. It is easy to lie to oneself. One of the things that we can lie about is the degree to which our reaction to Watergate was merely rational, not emotional, and yet anyone who remembers those days will also remember the strong emotions aroused by everything that happened. When I think of this part of our story, I am reminded of words of Edmund Burke:

You see, Sir, that in this enlightened age I am bold enough to confess that we are generally men of untaught feelings, that, instead of casting away all our old prejudices, we cherish them to a considerable degree, and, to take more shame to ourselves, we cherish them because they are prejudices; and the longer they have lasted and the more generally they have prevailed, the more we cherish them. We are afraid to put men to live and trade each on his own private stock of reason, because we suspect that this stock in each man is small, and that the individuals would do better to avail themselves of the general bank and capital of nations and ages.

There is much in this passage that seems true about our reaction to Watergate, even though the tone of the passage is distinctly foreign to our sensibilities. The fear of individual initiative sounds wrong, for we live in a culture that honors individualism. But what rings true about it, as a description of the way we responded to Watergate, is that Richard Nixon seemed to offend our deepest sensibilities, our "prejudices," about right and wrong. We would not say nowadays that prejudices are "untaught," for we know that they are; but we also know that the most important teaching is the nonformal, almost subliminal kind, and so Burke is only slightly off target here. "Not consciously taught" is perhaps more accurate than "untaught."

Burke's sentences remind us that we need to look beyond the immediate issues into the passions that lie beneath them. The point to be made is that we are all too likely, when speaking of political events, to focus on the issues that become the explicit points for debate. For example, in the days of the Watergate affair, there was an extended debate about the facts. It quickly became established that crimes had been committed. But did Nixon know about them? Did he approve? And so there was a debate about who said what to whom and when—for it is out of details such as these that one constructs the chain of inferences about what appear to have been the facts.

Factual debates of this sort are understandable, indeed important. When we act, we ought to act on a correct understanding of the facts. However, there are some dangers in letting ourselves be swept up in the debate about the facts, for in doing so we can lose sight of the issue. After all, facts are important to us because they are relevant to something that we care about. But we should ask what that something is—what we *do* care about, and why.

If we ask these questions, Burke is a useful reminder to us, for he cautions us to look in the right place. He reminds us that our "untaught feelings" are crucial. To be sure, there was rational argument about the evidence; but there was also passion. Not only does Burke remind us to remember that passion has its place in politics, he also asks us not to be ashamed of this fact. Indeed, the major point of his essay is that a politics governed solely by either passion or reason is bound to be a bad politics; the only healthy politics is one in which reason and passion are yoked together so as to strengthen each other.

I have quoted two sentences from Burke. I would now like to quote the two that follow next:

Many of our men of speculation, instead of exploding general prejudices, employ their sagacity to discover the latent wisdom which prevail in them. If they find what they seek, and they seldom fail, they think it more important to continue the prejudice, with the reason involved, than to cast away the coat of prejudice and to leave nothing but the naked reason; because prejudice, with its reason, has a motive to give action to that reason, and an affection which will give it permanence.

There is a lesson in this passage, if we can get past the parts that offend our own sensibilities, the "prejudices" that we hold to so firmly. None of us would want to say, nowadays, that we would expect to find, on examining our prejudices, that they are rational. Nor would we say that we are unwilling "to cast away the coat of prejudice" and rely on the reason that underlies it. Even so, the fact remains that we hold deep prejudices that were offended by Nixon and his associates. The rest of the world did not seem to be offended in the way that we were. If one judges what we did by cosmopolitan and international standards, our response to what we learned about Watergate, our sense of disgust with all of it, was parochial and narrow. How then can we justify our revulsion, except by examining our prejudices for the "latent wisdom" that might lie within? At any rate, this is what I would like to do. But I differ from Burke; I fear that our "latent wisdom" may also be folly.

In this book I shall focus primarily on what thirty-eight people said, the thirty-eight who were members of the House Judiciary

Committee. Of course, these members of Congress were statistically unrepresentative; their social class and income ran well
above the average, and they were all trained as lawyers. Indeed, it
would be hard to imagine a group that would be less typical of the
country, although it could be argued that they were ideal as a "jury of
one's peers" for Richard Milhous Nixon. However, these thirty-eight
individuals were our legal representatives. They had the legal and
constitutional power to speak on our behalf. We could write letters
to them, and we could try to affect the course of opinion in our
communities, hoping that changes there might affect them in turn.
Yet even if we were successful our language would be translated by
them into their own tongue. Even though our words could have a
part in shaping and reshaping our polity, their words were important
in some special way, for it was they who occupied the strategically
important position.

Consequently, I suspect that their words might have a historical
importance that should make us wary. If we ever go through this
process again, it might be that our successors will look back to what
these thirty-eight men and women did, reread what they said, and
take their positions as a precedent. Would we want that? Did our
representatives represent us? Did they say what we would have had
them say, understand it as we understood it, give it the meaning that
we would have had them give it? And further, if we do object, can we
do anything about it?

I have been asking the question: "If this is the way we talk, who are
we?" I could amend this question to read: "As for the members of the
Judiciary Committee, if this is the way they talked, who were they?"
But I don't want to amend it in this way, for if I ask it thus, it sounds
too personal, too psychological; I do not wish to invade their psyches.
I did not choose them from out of the millions who talked because I
find them to be personally striking, but because of the constitutional
and legal fact that they represented us. So the question must go something like this: "If they represented us, and if they talked this way,
then what did they represent us to be?" If this is the question, then we
should be concerned with the answer, for we should care whether
they misrepresented us or told the truth about us.

2 CHRONOLOGY

The first step toward understanding what was said is to put it in context, which can be done by telling part of the story, by giving enough of the chronology so that one may have a better feel for the events of which our representatives spoke. The retelling of this often-told story is not merely desirable, it is necessary. The events that we know as Watergate are in the past now, and memory has begun to fade. Just as time brings a loss of memory, it also brings something good, new citizens too young to remember or else not then born. Consequently, I think it good to set forth a brief chronology, to remind the old and inform the young.

The dates that mark off the bounds of this chronology are June 17, 1972, when the burglary occurred, a burglary of the headquarters of the Democratic National Committee, and August 9, 1974, when Nixon gave his farewell speech following his resignation. In the beginning, it was inconceivable that the burglary would have the important consequences that were to follow. At first, the burglary seemed minor enough so that the editors of the *Washington Post* assigned Bob Woodward to cover it; he was young (twenty-nine years old) and a relatively inexperienced reporter. Woodward was soon joined on the story by Carl Bernstein, who was slightly more experienced as a reporter, even though he was a year younger. Their work on the story would make them famous, but if the editors had had any suspicions of where the story might lead, they would not have put these two men in charge of it.

At the time, there was no way that the editors could have known. Even though it was an election year, so that one would expect some political "dirty tricks," still it did not seem likely that a felony such

as burglary would be part of the routine of campaigning. Such a felony would seem beyond the boundary of the rough-and-tumble of
politics. In their book, *All the President's Men,* Woodward and Bernstein stated that they too did not imagine, at the outset, that the
burglary was linked to larger political events:

> Indeed, the thought that the break-in might somehow be the work of the
> Republicans seemed implausible. On June 17, 1972, less than a month be-
> fore the Democratic convention, the President stood ahead of all announced
> Democratic candidates in the polls by no less than 19 points. Richard Nix-
> on's vision of an emerging Republican majority that would dominate the
> last quarter of a century, much as the Democrats had dominated two pre-
> vious generations, appeared possible. The Democratic Party was in disarray
> as a brutal primary season approached its end. Senator George McGovern of
> South Dakota, considered by the White House and Democratic Party profes-
> sionals alike to be Nixon's weakest opponent, was emerging as the clear
> favorite to win the Democrats' nomination for President.

As it turned out, McGovern was in fact nominated, and the profes-
sionals' judgment about the likely outcome of the campaign was
vindicated: Nixon beat McGovern about as decisively as is possible.

At the time, the only things that we could know were a few facts
about those who broke into the Democratic headquarters. Three of
the men—Bernard Barker, Virgilio Gonzales, and Eugene Martinez—had been born in Cuba and were living in Miami as part of the
Cuban exile community. Apparently, some of them had been par-
tisans in Castro's movement, but they had become anti-Castro. Another member of the group was Frank Sturgis, who was born in Nor-
folk, Virginia, and who was reputed to be a soldier-of-fortune type.
The early speculation, which proved to be accurate, was that the
four of them had been involved in anti-Castro activities sponsored
by the CIA. But this sort of speculation was not widespread among
the citizenry; it was limited to Washington insiders.

The leader of the group was James McCord. For twenty years
(1951–71) he had worked for the CIA, and before that he had worked
for the FBI. After retiring from the CIA in 1971, he set himself up in
business as a "security consultant." (The legitimate side of this sort
of business is the giving of advice to those who need to protect
themselves against bugging or burglary.) All of these facts were

mildly interesting, but the important fact was that he was a security coordinator for the Committee to Re-elect the President (CREEP).

This fact—that McCord was a security coordinator for CREEP—immediately became ambiguous. John Mitchell, the director of the committee, put out a statement that obfuscated the point:

The person involved is the proprietor of a private security agency who was employed by our committee months ago to assist with the installation of our security system. He has, as we understand it, a number of business clients and interests, and we have no knowledge of these relationships. We want to emphasize that this man and the other people involved were not operating on either our behalf or with our consent. There is no place in our campaign or in the electoral process for this type of activity, and we will not permit or condone it.

The statement implied, without stating directly, that McCord was not a full-time employee of CREEP but instead had been merely a consultant. However, when the reporters talked to McCord's friends, they all said that he worked full time for the committee. Since McCord was not giving interviews, there was no way to get his version. Of course, there were business records that could have been used to settle the matter, but reporters do not have the power to compel anyone to produce such records. All these things meant that McCord's actual relationship to the committee was unclear.

The case began in the Metropolitan Police Department, but the investigation was soon taken over by the FBI. The technicalities of bureaucratic jurisdiction—who investigates what—are complicated in this sort of case because of the District of Columbia's special status as a federal enclave; the details of these arrangements change from time to time, and are not today what they were at the time of Watergate.

The newspaper reports on the day after the burglary stated that the burglars had intended to set up a "bugging operation," but the reports did not suggest who was behind the plot to bug the headquarters of the Democratic National Committee. The story was a front-page one, but it made the front page because of the importance of the victim, the Democratic National Committee; the burglars themselves were not front-page individuals. Within two more days, however, there was a headline in the *Washington Post:* "White House

Consultant Linked to Bugging Suspects." Howard Hunt, the consultant, was listed in the address books of two of the suspects. Within six weeks, by the end of July and the start of August, stories appeared in the *Post* in which a financial link was established: checks that had been contributed to the Nixon campaign had been deposited in the bank account of one of the suspects. A Government Accounting Office (GAO) investigation followed up on those charges and corroborated the essentials of the story.

The GAO report did not focus on links to the Watergate break-in. Instead, the investigators looked for violations of the Federal Election Campaign Act of 1971, and they reported five "apparent" and four "possible" violations of that act: these were failures to keep records and make reports. Charges of this sort sound merely technical and therefore did not seem significant. The most dramatic fact that was revealed in the report was the existence of a $350,000 cash fund that was kept in a safe in Maurice Stans's office. Stans was in charge of fundraising for CREEP, and so it was not unusual for him to have control of large sums of money. However, there is no reason to keep cash in a private safe unless one wishes to avoid leaving the sort of "paper trail" that bank accounts, deposit slips, and checks are sure to leave. One doesn't keep cash like that lying around without some reason, a troubling reason. The GAO report was more significant than the newspaper stories about Howard Hunt. The latter were ambiguous, in that one could doubt what inferences to draw from them. The status of "consultant" is unclear; what was his relationship to important people in the White House? Nor was it clear whether he had merely once been a consultant or was still a consultant. The financial link between the burglars and CREEP was far more significant.

However, the indictments that were filed in the middle of September 1972 were limited in their scope: they focused on the burglary, the unlawful entry with intent to "bug", but they did not do more; Howard Hunt and Gordon Liddy were added to the initial five as defendants, but they were political operators and had nothing to do with the money. Perhaps the prosecutors had reason to think this was good strategy, but by omitting any details about how the defendants were funded, the prosecutors caused many people to become even more suspicious. Wright Patman, who chaired the House Banking and Currency Committee, was one of the suspicious. He tried to start a probe into the campaign finances of Nixon's reelection campaign; but on October 3, 1972, six of the Democrats joined the fourteen Republicans on his committee to vote down by a 20–15 vote any probe into campaign finances.

At this point the members of Congress cease to be actors. An election was approaching, and there would soon be a new Congress and a reelected president. The center of any talk and action was in the press, where stories about foul play in the campaign began to appear, and in the judiciary, where the processes of criminal procedure moved along in their stately way. The matter received sustained attention in the press, but the revelations about Watergate were limited, and there was no damage to the Nixon campaign. Even when the *Washington Post* reported, on October 10, 1972, that CREEP had been directing a wide-ranging campaign of espionage and dirty tricks against the Democrats, this report did not seem to affect public opinion. The story described such dirty tricks as forging letters on stationery that bore Democratic letterheads, leaking false information to the press, and also acts that went beyond the dirty-tricks category—for example, theft of confidential files. Aside from legalities and illegalities, the nastiest act was forging a letter that charged Sen. Edmund Muskie with having spoken of Americans of French-Canadian descent as "Canucks," a letter that had damaged Muskie's campaign to be the Democratic nominee for president.

All these things appeared to be linked to the Watergate break-in, but it was not clear exactly what was the link. According to the newspapers, the link was financial, in that the sabotage operations were paid for from a secret cash fund, and so was the break-in. However, it was not yet clear who controlled these funds, how they operated, and so forth, and until it could be shown that all of the acts uncovered were directed by the same group of people, there was not much that could be made of them. The suspicious among us thought that these new revelations were to be connected with the earlier reporting, but the general public was not suspicious. In November 1972 Richard Nixon was reelected in a landslide.

In January 1973 the trial of the Watergate burglars began in the

U.S. District Court for the District of Columbia. John Sirica was the chief judge of the court at that time, and he assigned the case to himself. Hunt, Barker, Sturgis, Martinez, and Gonzalez pleaded guilty. Whenever a defendant pleads guilty, the judge must ask questions to find out if the plea is truly voluntary and rests upon an accurate understanding of the exact nature of the charges and of what the consequences of the guilty plea will be. Sirica tried to use this procedure to make public what had happened, but defense counsel objected to the judge's questions on the grounds that the defendants were still under investigation for other matters; the objection was legally proper, and so Sirica, with visible reluctance, abandoned his inquiry.

Liddy and McCord pleaded not guilty and the trial went forward against them; they were convicted. The trial itself became one of the notable events of that January, largely because of Sirica's actions. The lawyers were focusing upon the question of guilt or innocence with respect to the break-in, but Sirica intervened from time to time to ask questions about the other matters that were relevant to the overall problem. Within the legal community, there was considerable criticism of Sirica, since many lawyers thought that this sort of judicial intervention was not part of his proper role as a judge. The argument was that he should have limited himself to the trial before him. However, the general public seemed to approve, perhaps because this was the first chance for facts about Watergate to be made public in some sort of regular and authorized manner. There was a real desire to know the truth, and this was the first public hearing on the truth about Watergate. At any rate, despite Sirica's attempts, nothing much came out and so the focus of the action returned to the legislative arena; it was time for a new Congress to meet.

While the trial was under way, the new Congress (the Ninety-third) convened, and our representatives once again had a chance to act. After the customary and expected to'ing and fro'ing, the first significant act came on February 7, 1973: the Senate Select Committee on Presidential Campaign Activities, more popularly known as the Ervin committee, was established. The public curiosity for knowledge about Watergate was so great that not a single senator opposed an investigation; the vote was 77–0. Sen. Sam Ervin had to put together a staff and get organized, and so for a couple of months there was not much from that quarter.

For the moment, the initiative on Capitol Hill was taken up by the Senate Judiciary Committee. On February 28, 1973, this committee began the confirmation hearing on Patrick Gray's nomination as head of the FBI. The committee members used this opportunity to ask Gray about what he had done to investigate the numerous allegations of foul play. The senators used some creative ingenuity in stretching out the hearings; and the longer they went on, the more Gray's answers made him look like part of a conspiracy to obstruct justice instead of the investigator who was supposed to be breaking up such a conspiracy.

The parts of Gray's testimony that were most damaging to him were his admissions that he had let John Dean sit in on FBI interviews of White House officials and that he had turned over FBI files to Dean. John Dean's official title was counsel to the president. According to Nixon's public statements, Dean was supposed to be investigating, on the president's behalf, whether any members of the White House had been involved in criminality. When Gray went on to say that he thought Dean had lied to the FBI when he said that he didn't know Hunt had an office in the White House, then he was through. It was bad enough to turn over files to Dean, but to do so while believing him to be a liar was absurd. On April 5, 1973, Nixon withdrew Gray's nomination.

Within the month, matters got worse for Gray. On April 26 the *New York Daily News* reported that he had destroyed documents that had belonged to Hunt, including some phony State Department cables that Hunt had fabricated to implicate President Kennedy in the 1963 assassination of Ngo Dihn Diem, premier of South Vietnam. Why would the director of the FBI destroy evidence? On April 27, Gray resigned.

The documents in question came from Howard Hunt's safe, which was in an office in the Executive Office Building (the workplace for the president's staff). Three days after the Watergate burglary, John Dean had opened this safe and taken from it documents that linked

Hunt to other "dirty tricks", including other burglaries. Patrick Gray was the acting director of the FBI at this time, and Dean turned the documents over to him. Six months later, Gray destroyed them.

Gray attempted to portray his acts as merely impulsive gestures of misplaced loyalty, and not fundamentally corrupt, but this sort of defense doesn't work too well. All of these revelations made quite a problem for Nixon, who had to decide whether to condemn Gray or to continue to support him and try to justify what he had done. John Ehrlichman's solution, which was leaked to the press, was: "[L]et him hang there. Let him twist slowly, slowly in the wind." And in fact, this was more or less what happened; they did nothing, and so Gray resigned without having received much in the way of either support or condemnation from Nixon.

While this was going on, the day for sentencing in the criminal trial came up. The significant event of that day, March 23, 1973, was Sirica's making public a letter that McCord had written to him. In this letter McCord said that there had been political pressure on the defendants to plead guilty and keep silent and that there had been perjury in the trial. Sirica imposed "provisional" maximum sentences on several of the defendants, and he made it clear that he would consider whether they cooperated with the prosecutors when it came time to impose the actual sentences. It was obvious that Liddy would never cooperate, and so Sirica gave him a stiff sentence. Sentencing for McCord was postponed.

Subsequently, McCord began to talk to the staff of the Ervin committee, and on April 5, Sirica gave him immunity from further prosecution so that he would testify before the grand jury. (The phrase "immunity from *further* prosecution" has a particular technical meaning. McCord, who had pleaded not guilty, wished to appeal his conviction. If he had won his appeal, he could have been retried. His dilemma was that any statements made before the committee could have been used at the retrial. And thus the immunity: he could make statements without the risk that they would be used against him, if there was a retrial. But the conviction was affirmed, and so it turned out to be unimportant.) The newspapers began to carry "McCord says" stories: that John Mitchell, who had once been attorney general of the United States, and who had been director of the president's campaign, had approved the break-in, for example.

In the middle of the month, April 17, 1973, Nixon finally changed his position with reference to the Ervin committee. Previously, he had insisted that his aides would not testify, asserting "executive privilege" as the purported legal basis for this position. Now he changed ground and said that they would appear. He also made a second statement, which was rather opaque and mysterious, that there had been new developments in the case but that he couldn't say what they were. Within two days the attorney general, Richard Kleindienst, said that he was disqualifying himself from any further participation in the case so that he would not have to prosecute any of his colleagues in the Nixon administration. The Gray testimony and the McCord letter, together with other matters that were in the press, before and after, created a rather significant problem for the president. So far as I know, we do not yet have a complete account of the political dynamics of the first four months of 1973, and I know that I could not write such an account; but for the purpose of this book, it is clear enough what the most significant public acts were: on April 27, 1973, Patrick Gray resigned as acting director of the FBI; this step was followed on April 30 by the resignations of H. R. Haldeman as White House chief of staff, of John Ehrlichman as chief of domestic affairs, of John Dean as counsel to the president, and of Richard Kleindienst as attorney general of the United States.

An obvious question in the public mind was: why did they all resign so precipitously? By this time, suspicions were such that most people did not accept the publicly declared reasons as the whole truth, even if they were true. Kleindienst said that people "with whom I had close personal and professional associations" were suspects and that therefore he should not serve as attorney general. If this is accepted as the reason, then he resigned so as to avoid the appearance of impropriety. Haldeman and Ehrlichman said that the attacks made upon them and the rumors that they had participated in the cover-up had made it impossible for them to do their jobs, because they would have to spend too many hours refuting falsehoods and establishing the truth. If this is accepted as the reason, then they resigned in order to participate in the search for truth and so that the administrative operation of the White House could proceed efficiently. Even if all these things were true, there were also other problems. It was no longer possible for anyone to believe the story that White House officials had originally told; it was no longer plausible to contend that Hunt and Liddy had acted on their own, without any authority from those who were higher up.

The Kleindienst resignation gave the Senate Judiciary Committee another confirmation hearing with which to work. The nominee himself, Elliot Richardson, was untainted by the whole affair and had impeccable credentials; thus the "Gray gambit" was not available. However, the senators were able to get some concessions in exchange for confirmation; Richardson agreed to set up a special prosecutor to investigate Watergate, and he appointed Archibald Cox to that position. After this step, the focus of public attention shifted to the Ervin committee.

Of all the congressional action preceding that of the House Judiciary Committee, there is no doubt that the Ervin committee was the most important. Its hearings began on May 17, 1973, and lasted most of the summer. The scope of the inquiry, as a simple quantitative fact, is enough to have made what the committee did important. Furthermore, its impact on the political dynamics was extraordinary.

The first witness to say anything that confirmed the newspaper speculation was Hugh Sloan, who had been treasurer of the finance committee of CREEP and who testified on June 6 and 7. Sloan told of the large sums of money that came into the committee in cash (not by check) and of large cash disbursements. He said that $199,000 had been given to Liddy, that he had been asked by Fred LaRue and Jeb Magruder to lie about this sum and say that it was only $40,000, and that he had been asked by John Dean to conceal it by claiming the privilege against self-incrimination. Rather than lie or claim the Fifth, Sloan resigned. This testimony was important, for it was the first public testimony, under oath, that presented evidence about what lay behind the Watergate affair. To be sure, it was but one small piece in the puzzle, but it was crucial: it was solid information that large sums of money were involved and that powerful men were afraid of having the truth made public.

Although Hugh Sloan's testimony was damaging, it was limited in its scope. During the week of June 25–29, John Dean took the stand, and his story was not a narrowly limited one. Dean's title, when he worked at the White House, had been counsel to the president, but this imposing title conceals more than it reveals, since it was not clear to anyone just what sort of counsel Dean was supposed to give to the president. Dean was not a political counselor; it was well-known that Nixon did not meet with Dean in order to get political advice. It was said that he handled legal problems, but what kind? Important legal questions (whether the executive should assert that a proposed bill in the Congress was unconstitutional, or how the executive should respond to cases filed in court) were handled by lawyers who worked at the Justice Department. Nixon might reject the counsel of these lawyers, but he did so for political reasons and without asking Dean about it. On the other hand, Dean did not advise Nixon about his personal legal problems (tax returns, real estate transactions), for these were handled by Herbert Kalmbach, who was a partner in a Los Angeles law firm. In short, it appeared that John Dean, despite his fancy title, was fairly insignificant. However, his testimony turned out to be highly significant. His story was that various members of the White House staff had worked together to frustrate the FBI investigation of the events that had led up to the Watergate burglary, that he himself had been one of the chief architects of this conspiracy, and that Nixon knew what was happening and had approved.

Through the rest of the summer, there was a parade of witnesses, and the event caught the imagination of the nation. Those who had once held power, but now had left office, were subpoenaed to give their versions. The big names were Mitchell, Ehrlichman, and Haldeman. In different ways, each of them contradicted Dean, although their several stories were by no means mutually consistent. Indeed, since there was no way to put together the various versions so as to get a coherent narrative of what had happened, the significance of what they said about the particulars of Dean's story was far less important than some of the by-ways of the hearings.

For example, John Mitchell testified that he did not approve of the break-in, but that he did participate in the cover-up, and that he concealed from the president what he was doing. Although Mitchell made admissions that were damaging to himself, he did not create the impression that he was trying to tell the truth. He volunteered nothing, limiting his answers to the minimum necessary response. He was noncooperative in a way that expressed contempt. Consequently, one was left with the impression that what he had done was even worse than what he admitted to having done.

John Ehrlichman was not taciturn; he was highly verbal. The drama of his testimony was not in the factual assertions that he made but in the legal claims that he announced. Early on in his testimony, he spoke of his role in approving Liddy's break-in at the office of the psychiatrist who treated Daniel Ellsberg. In his testimony he drew a nice distinction. He admitted that he had approved of a covert action to get the medical files, but he said that he had not meant to approve burglary. Instead, he said that he thought Liddy would get the information by way of corrupting a nurse's aide, or something like that. What was spectacular about Ehrlichman's testimony, however, was that his real complaint with Liddy was not the fact of the burglary but that Liddy had not asked for his approval. Had approval been asked for and given, it would have been proper, according to Ehrlichman. In the most combative way, he claimed that it was necessary for reasons of national security to get these medical files, and therefore it was permissible. This assertion set off a memorable confrontation between Ehrlichman and Ervin, in which the senator thundered at him like an Old Testament prophet, like one who had come to condemn those who had fallen away from the law.

By way of contrast, H. R. Haldeman was soft-spoken and courteous. He had been the most powerful of the three, but his demeanor was the meekest. This too made a dramatic impression, for his reputation had been that he was ruthless. Indeed, the very mildness of his manner seemed to provoke disbelief, and so the senators questioned him sharply and vigorously, with a sense of frustration and astonishment.

When it was all through, the several stories left so many questions unanswered, and so many disputes unresolved, that the most important testimony was that of a man who had nothing to do with any of the events. Alexander Butterfield had been one of those who had responsibility for keeping records in the White House. He testified that all of Nixon's conversations with anyone in his office in the White House or the Executive Office Building had been taped (as were all of his telephone calls). Consequently, Butterfield raised the possibility of a source of evidence that could corroborate or refute the testimony of other witnesses.

Butterfield's disclosure preceded the testimony of the "big three," but their testimony made his seem even more important than it originally had. In my judgment of the political dynamics, the crucial events of these hearings were the spectacular accusation made by John Dean as he testified from June 25–29, 1973, and the testimony of Alexander Butterfield on July 16 that there were tapes. If Dean's accusations were believed, then Richard Nixon was guilty of a felony. In his testimony Dean gave an elaborate and detailed account of his conversations with Nixon, reporting on what he had said to Nixon and on what Nixon had said to him. Dean testified that he told Nixon what was being done to obstruct the investigation into Watergate, and he further testified that Nixon approved of what was done and implied that he was to do more. The joint testimony of Butterfield and Dean was significant in ways that either by itself would not have been. Without Dean's testimony, the tapes would have been irrelevant. Without the tapes, Dean's word would have stood alone. However, the Ervin committee could not do much in response to what was said. It was commissioned to be an investigator; it had no real power to take action. Consequently, the scene had to shift from the Senate to the House.

As a matter of historical fact, before the scene shifted to the House, it shifted away from Capitol Hill. A battle began in the courts to get the tapes. Butterfield stated on July 16 that the tapes existed, and the first step in the legal battle was prompt; on July 23 the special prosecutor, Archibald Cox, took the first step. The legal minuet went as follows: a subpoena was issued; the president said he would not honor it; the judge said that he should show cause why he would not honor the subpoena; the president's lawyer filed a brief; the special prosecutor filed a brief; there were arguments; and so forth. It was all reasonably prompt, by standards of the law, yet it was also stately in its pace, as minuets always are. On August 29, 1973, Judge Sirica ruled against the president, and on October 12, 1973, the court of appeals affirmed this ruling.

Nixon did not want to accept his legal defeats; his way of stopping the special prosecutor from enforcing his victory was to fire him. The maneuvers by way of which Archibald Cox was fired were rather complicated. Nixon tried to come up with a way of giving a partial disclosure of the tapes, persuading the key political actors to accept this compromise, and then isolating Cox, so that he would have no allies if he chose to object. The proposal was to have one of the distinguished senior members of the Senate, John Stennis of Mississippi, listen to the tapes and verify that the transcripts of them that had been prepared in the White House were accurate. The scheme was partially successful, for such respected men as Attorney General Richardson and Senator Ervin agreed to it, although Ervin has claimed that it was not accurately described to him. However, Stennis never agreed, for he was hard of hearing and could not do it; and Archibald Cox objected, for it was clear under the rules of evidence that the edited transcripts would not be admissible in court and thus that they would be useless to him.

Faced with Cox's refusal, Nixon ordered Richardson to fire Cox, but Richardson refused to do so, even though he had agreed to the so-called Stennis compromise. Richardson said that he had promised Cox independence and that he would not go back on that promise. Consequently, Richardson resigned. Nixon next turned to the number-two man at the Department of Justice, Deputy Attorney General William Ruckelshaus, and ordered him to fire Cox. Ruckelshaus refused and submitted his resignation. The number-three man in the chain of command, Robert Bork, was willing to follow orders, and so he accepted the responsibility and fired Cox. All of this happened on October 20, 1973, and the events were dubbed the "Saturday Night Massacre." There were approximately a half million telegrams sent to Washington in protest. In response, the chairman of the House Judiciary Committee, Rep. Peter Rodino announced four days after the firing of Cox that the House Judiciary Committee would begin hearings on whether Richard Milhous Nixon should be impeached.

The next detail of chronology is to account for the three months leading up to January 31, 1974, which was the day the Judiciary Committee began meeting on Watergate. There was, of course, the work of assembling a staff and getting organized. But there was another problem: the vice-president, Spiro Agnew, had to resign (owing to straight, old-fashioned corruption, unconnected with Watergate); Gerald Ford was nominated on October 12 to be his successor. The first order of business for the Judiciary Committee was therefore to hold hearings on the Ford nomination. That was reasonable enough: it is not prudent to set about impeaching a president without having a vice-president in place.

At any rate, the committee members started to talk about Watergate, and their talk was different from all the other talk on the subject. All of their talk was connected to a necessity—they had to vote on impeachment. On January 31, 1974, the hearings began; six months later, on July 27, 29, and 30, 1974, they voted on articles of impeachment.

At its first meeting the committee approved a draft of a resolution which was to be passed by the House of Representatives authorizing the investigation. By February 6 the staff had begun briefing the committee members, and they got down to work fighting out the many questions of substance and procedure. Gathering the relevant evidence took approximately four months. By May 9, the staff for the committee were satisfied that all the relevant documents had been assembled, and for the next month and a half John Doar, who was the committee's counsel, began the tedious job of leading the members through the documents. At the end of June the committee decided which witnesses to call, and from July 2 through July 17, 1974, the committee heard the testimony of witnesses. There followed several days of summation of counsel, and then on July 24 two significant events took place. On that day the Supreme Court handed down its opinion in the case of *United States* v. *Nixon*, in which it decided that the special prosecutor, who was by this time Leon Jaworski, was entitled to receive the tapes that Archibald Cox had been asking for. On that same day the members of the House Judiciary Committee began their opening statements; each one made a statement, and it took two days to get through them. On July

26 and 27 the committee debated what was to become Article I of the resolution of impeachment. The debate on July 29 was on Article II, and on July 30 the committee wound up voting on the rest of the matters before it.

There were five different articles of impeachment submitted to a vote; three were passed and two were defeated. All of the hearings and arguments led up to these votes. At this point in the chronology, I would like to be rather detailed, since I know that most do not know the exact nature of the charges. My own experience has been that even those people who are most hostile in their memory of Nixon cannot say what it is that he was charged with having done; even those who are sure that he was guilty cannot specify the crime. Consequently, it is important to be precise.

To repeat, then: five articles of impeachment were submitted to a vote; on three the vote was yes (impeach) and on two the vote was no. In the following list, the first three articles are the ones for which the vote was yes. That is, these are the articles that the committee was willing to carry to the House of Representatives with a recommendation that the House vote to impeach Nixon for them. If the process had gone that far (if Nixon had not resigned), then these would have been the articles on which Nixon might have been tried in the Senate, on which he might have been convicted, and for which he might have been removed from office. The charges and the votes were:

   I.   Obstruction of justice: 27 ayes, 11 nays
   II. Abuse of power: 28 ayes, 10 nays
   III. Defying subpoenas: 21 ayes, 17 nays
   IV. Concealing bombing: 12 ayes, 26 nays
   V.   Emoluments and tax fraud: 12 ayes, 26 nays

The first article did not actually bear the title "obstruction of justice"; this is merely the shorthand description of it. As we all know, there was a burglary of the national headquarters of the Democratic party in the Watergate apartment complex; an investigation started; there was a conspiracy to obstruct the investigation. Article I charged that Richard Nixon was a party to this conspiracy and therefore should be impeached.

Article II dealt with Nixon's use of executive power for improper purposes; for example, it was charged that he ordered the IRS to conduct tax audits with the intention of intimidating his political enemies. There were other examples fitting this general pattern of misuse of power.

In order to investigate, the committee had to gather evidence; in an attempt to do so, subpoenas were issued to the president. His refusal to comply was charged as an impeachable offense in Article III. The yes vote on this article, as is clear from the numbers given, was a close one.

During the Vietnam war, Nixon ordered the bombing of Cambodia; however, he concealed this operation and had false statements submitted to the Congress about it. These lies were charged as an impeachable offense in Article IV.

And finally, there was a charge of straight, old-fashioned corruption. Nixon had his home in San Clemente improved at government expense, and he took some tax deductions that he was not entitled to take. These acts of personal self-enrichment and tax fraud were charged as impeachable offenses under Article V. (The label "Article V" is mine; it was not so identified by the committee.)

Our problem is deciding how one ought to talk about these charges, but the pattern of the votes raises an additional issue: not merely what was said about each of them individually, but how they were distinguished. What reasons can be offered for voting no to two of the articles while voting yes to three others?

Suppose the bombing and the burglary were both illegal. Is not illegal bombing worse than illegal burglary? But the vote goes the other way. One might distinguish by describing the bombing as basically a political issue, the burglary as a legal issue, and then arguing that impeachment ought to be based on legal standards. However, the tax evasion was clearly a legal offense, and yet here the vote was no; and the abuse of power seems more political than legal, and yet the vote was yes. How do we make sense of this pattern? How did the members of the judiciary committee make sense of it?

Since the pattern of votes seems so important, we should take a closer look. There were eight Democrats who voted yes all five times and ten Republicans who voted no all five times. This left thirteen Democrats and seven Republicans whose votes varied. In the accompanying chart, the Democrats are listed first, in five groups, according to their pattern of voting and in order of seniority; the Republicans are broken down into four groups.

The information in this chart can be summarized as follows: The two blocks of "straight-ticket" votes gave a two-vote edge to no, but clearly the middle group of twenty was decisive. The middle column is Article III, the subpoena; as noted, this was the closest vote. Only two Democrats, Flowers and Mann, voted no. There were still enough votes to impeach, but two Republicans, McClory and Hogan, joined the yes side to increase the margin from two to four votes. The two outer columns might be called the "legal" articles: I is the conspiracy to obstruct justice and V is the personal enrichment and tax-fraud charge. Of the middle group of twenty, only one, McClory, voted no to I; only four, Rodino, Eilberg, Sieberling, and Danielson, voted yes to V. So the margins were decisive: 27 to 11, 12 to 26. II and IV might be called the "political" articles. The entire middle group voted yes to II, but only four, Hungate, Waldie, Drinan, and Owens, voted yes to IV. Once again, the margins were decisive: 28 to 10, 12 to 26.

Note the interesting anomaly in the votes on IV and V: although the middle supplied only four yes votes on each article, it was a completely different group of four each time. And McClory's pattern of votes is especially interesting; he voted no on I and yes on II and III.

After the votes were taken, the denouement was fairly quick. On the last day of voting, July 30, the delivery of the tapes to Judge Sirica began. Counsel for the president, James St. Clair, had himself not listened to these tapes. After he did, he had the leading Republican defenders also listen to them, especially the crucial tape of June 23, 1972, which recorded conversations made six days after the Watergate break-in. In this tape the president instructed his chief of staff, H. R. Haldeman, to ask the CIA to interfere with the FBI's investigation. On August 5 the transcript of this tape was made public and the defenders ceased defending. On August 9 Nixon resigned.

This ends the chronology, and thus the introductory parts of this book. I now wish to turn to the words of the thirty-eight men and women of the House Judiciary Committee and ask if they repre-

	ARTICLES				
	I	II	III	IV	V
DEMOCRATS					
Jack Brooks, Tex.; Robert W. Kastenmeier, Wis.; Don Edwards, Calif.; John Conyers, Jr., Mich.; Charles B. Rangel, N.Y.; Barbara Jordan, Tex.; Elizabeth Holtzman, N.Y.; Edward Mezvinsky, Iowa	yes	yes	yes	yes	yes
William L. Hungate, Mo.; Jerome R. Waldie, Calif.; Robert F. Drinan, Mass.; Wayne Owens, Utah	yes	yes	yes	yes	no
Peter W. Rodino, Jr., N.J.; Joshua Eilberg, Pa.; John F. Seiberling, Ohio; George E. Danielson, Calif.	yes	yes	yes	no	yes
Harold D. Donohue, Mass.; Paul S. Sarbanes, Md.; Ray Thornton, Ark.	yes	yes	yes	no	no
Walter Flowers, Ala.; James R. Mann, S.C.	yes	yes	no	no	no
REPUBLICANS					
Robert McClory, Ill.	no	yes	yes	no	no
Lawrence J. Hogan, Md.	yes	yes	yes	no	no
Rom Railsback, Ill.; Hamilton Fish, Jr., N.Y.; M. Caldwell Butler, Va.; William S. Cohen, Me.; Harold V. Froehlich, Wis.	yes	yes	no	no	no
Edward Hutchinson, Mich.; Henry P. Smith III, N.Y.; Charles W. Sandman, Jr., N.J.; Charles E. Wiggins, Calif.; David W. Dennis, Ind.; Wiley Mayne, Iowa; Trent Lott, Miss.; Carlos J. Moorhead, Calif.; Joseph J. Maraziti, N.J.; Delbert L. Latta, Ohio	no	no	no	no	no

sented us well, if they spoke as we would have had them speak. As I have already mentioned, all thirty-eight members of the Judiciary Committee were lawyers. We therefore can anticipate, and correctly so, that we will find their talk full of legal terms, that legal analogies came naturally to them. However, they were also politicians, and so they were also adept at speaking in public in nonlegal ways. Our problem is to understand how they combined the legal and the non-legal, and then we must decide whether we approve of what they said.

3 THE LEGAL IMAGINATION AT WORK

The transcript starts with Thursday, January 31, 1974, and it begins the way transcripts begin: "The committee met, pursuant to notice, at 10 a.m., in room 2141, Rayburn House Office Building, Hon. Peter W. Rodino, Jr. (chairman) presiding." Much had gone before. It was now time for the members of the House of Representatives to consider what their responsibilities were, and perhaps to act. Resolutions of impeachment had been introduced in the House and referred by the Speaker to the Judiciary Committee.

A staff of lawyers and investigators had been organized, plans had been made, and the members of the Judiciary Committee had assembled to get started. The chairman called upon the next senior member of the majority party, Representative Donohue, who said: "Mr. Chairman, I offer the following resolution and recommend that it be reported favorably to the full House." We are now, as the literary theorists say, *in medias res*, in the middle of it; the action is under way. Something has already been done, and it seems that the next action is to ask something called "the full House" to pass a resolution.

In other words, although these pages are the opening pages of the transcript, they are not the beginning of the Judiciary Committee's actions. At the very least, someone has drafted a resolution, and now the chairman and the senior member of the majority are executing a procedural ritual to put the resolution before the committee. I want to try to use their language as a set of clues concerning how they are thinking about the problem. As I have already said, they are lawyers, but they are also politicians; they use legal language, but it is not obvious what this fact means. The only way to proceed is to pay careful attention to the details of the language and try to read between the lines.

Consider the first two sentences of the proposed resolution:

Resolved, that the Committee on the Judiciary, acting as a whole or by any subcommittee thereof, is authorized and directed to investigate fully and completely whether sufficient grounds exist for the House of Representatives to exercise its constitutional power to impeach Richard M. Nixon, President of the United States of America. The committee shall report to the House of Representatives such resolutions, articles of impeachment or other recommendations as it deems proper.

Words like these are novel in their content but familiar to us in their form. The content, impeaching a president, is extraordinary, but otherwise the language is dull and routine and the procedure is normal. (How many times have members of a committee drafted a resolution upon which a legislature is to vote? It must be a countless number.) One could also say that this language, the first two sentences of the proposed resolution, has a legalistic sound, although we can't draw any large conclusions from this fact. The only thing that we can be sure of is that we have here a "convention," a rule of procedure; this convention provides that a resolution must be "introduced" before it can be debated and voted upon; Donohue, who is the senior Democrat after the chairman, is playing his part. Someone has to do something to get things started, and seniority is one way of picking out who the someone shall be. There is nothing magic or necessary about these particular rules of procedure, but some such rules are necessary.

Since the procedure is routine, one must be cautious in interpreting it; however, even the routine can be an important clue. Recall that the first sentence of the proposed resolution stated: "*Resolved*, that the Committee on the Judiciary, acting as a whole or by any subcommittee thereof, is authorized and directed to investigate fully and completely whether sufficient grounds exist for the House of Representatives to exercise its constitutional power to impeach Richard M. Nixon, President of the United States of America." It may be painful to linger over the details of such language, but it is worth doing so in order to be able to ask: is it not strange? It did not have to be written this way; there were other possibilities. Why did the drafter not say: "*Resolved*, that the Committee on the Judiciary shall investigate whether the President shall be impeached." The word "shall" is a word that commands, and surely "shall investigate" means the same thing as "is . . . directed to investigate." And if you are directed to do something, are you not authorized to do it? Would it not be incoherent to say to someone: "You are directed, but not authorized, to investigate . . ." So what sort of imagination produces the phrase "is authorized and directed to investigate"?

Furthermore, when you tell someone to investigate something, should you pick someone you trust? Do you feel the need to tell this person "to investigate fully and completely"? What do these two adverbs add? Would the investigation go differently without them? And why do we have the phrase "acting as a whole or by any subcommittee"? Why should a quibble like this be in a great paper of state? Does not the general parliamentary law handle such matters?

However, we must not get carried away with criticism; I suspect that most of us are more likely to say things like "is authorized and directed to investigate" than "shall investigate," and so the special role and circumstances in which the committee members spoke will not explain all that needs to be explained. Why is it that we are so likely to use bureaucratic prose rather than plain prose, even though it seems unnecessary? Partly it is no more than a linguistic osmosis: we are surrounded by bureaucratic prose, and so we begin to use it. More important, we often abandon the plain and simple style because we want to be circumspect, or perhaps especially serious; unless we are unusually skilled in making prose, our only linguistic mode (once the plain seems not subtle enough) may be the bureaucratic. Consequently, we are not surprised that the prose style of the resolution is stilted and bureaucratic.

Yet if bureaucratic or legalistic speech seems appropriate, there are still some problems of fitting it in with other things that we remember about Watergate. Those were days of passion; political arguments were heated. And so how does this bland speech square with that passion? One obvious suggestion is that this way of talking might be thought to be less dangerous than other possibilities. Politicians get wary when political arguments become passionate, and so Donohue, and his colleagues, might have chosen to speak "judiciously" because they might have hoped that it would be the safest way to speak. I can understand that choice, but there are perhaps other dangers that this style of language overlooks, and other objections that one could make.

Recall that the transcript, which begins on January 31, 1974, begins *in medias res.* A staff of investigators has been assembled, members have proposed various charges as grounds for impeachment, preliminary investigations have begun. Given this activity, a natural question for any member of the committee is: what is the relationship of this resolution to what has gone before?

The following colloquy between Caldwell Butler, a member, and John Doar, the special counsel for this investigation, is directed to the sentences that I have already quoted. (Note that Butler does not ask Donohue to answer his questions, and thus we can be confident that Donohue did not draft this resolution.)

Mr. Butler. Mr. Doar, addressing ourselves first to the reason for the preamble [the two sentences that begin the resolution]. This, as I view it, is a considerable enlargement of what I understood was the basis for your investigation to date. Am I correct in my recollection, that you have told us informally or formally on several occasions that you felt limited in your investigations to the charges that have been contained in the resolutions which were before this committee? Am I fair in that recollection?

Mr. Doar. In the preliminary inquiry, Congressman, we were investigating the charges that were in the resolutions before the committee, yes, that is right.

Mr. Butler. And so the effect of this is to enlarge, if we pass this resolution, is to enlarge the investigative power which you think that you have had up to the present, is this a fair statement?

Let us interrupt the colloquy. Note how simple the question is, and how basic. So far the investigation has been limited, although you and I as readers do not know the details of this limitation. However, they say that they have talked about this problem, and the transcript reads as though they have some shared understanding of the scope of the limitation. Given this background, the question seems to be important; here is the answer:

Mr. Doar. Well, I think that within the resolutions that were before the committee, there was authority to conduct a full and complete investigation into the question of whether or not there was sufficient grounds for this committee to recommend or not to recommend articles of impeachment to the House. I don't think that this resolution expands the power or the authority that this committee already has. I think what it does is confirms it and formalizes it, and this is the way in the past the House of Representatives has authorized and directed the Judiciary Committee to conduct an investigation.

What a remarkable answer! It is not apparent whether it is yes or no. In fact, the answer seems to deny the premise of the question, to which Doar has previously agreed, that the investigation to date has suffered under some limitation. What effect does the resolution have on the committee's authority? According to Doar, it does not expand authority, it doesn't even seem to grant authority; rather, it "confirms" and "formalizes." We must ask what these words mean, and whether we have here an example of ritual.

Butler did try to follow up on Doar's answer:

Mr. Butler. Then further, for my enlightenment, you really do not consider that [this preamble] is essential to the subpoena authority but it is for your purposes of clarifying and removing any doubt?

Mr. Doar. I think it is essential in the sense that I think it is important this this committee, in order to conduct a fair, full and expeditious investigation, fair to the President, fair to the Presidency and fair to the House of Representatives, that it have this authority explicitly stated by the House of Representatives.

Once again, the question is changed in its answering. By his question, Butler has moved from the topic of the scope of the investigation to the topic of subpoenas. The logic behind this move is to found in the law that governs subpoenas. Subpoenas can be issued by a committee so long as it is acting within the scope of its authority, but if the members try to investigate something that they are not authorized to investigate, then it follows (as a matter of legal theoretics) that their subpoenas are not legally valid. Given that Doar has said that the resolution is not a grant of authority to investigate, but is instead a confirmation and formalization, then it would seem to follow that the resolution is *not* crucial in any way to the question of the committee's authority to issue subpoenas. Consequently, this resolution might have some other function. In order to understand the point, Butler tries to gloss "confirm" and "formalize" by offering "clarify" and "remove any doubt" as substitute words, as translations that preserve equivalency in meaning. Butler's gloss seems plausible to me.

Doar does not answer the question; he escalates. Doar offers another translation, "to state explicitly," and he now declares that it is essential to "fairness." To make sense of his meaning demands an effort.

I am able to make sense out of Butler's question. Assuming that the resolution does not grant authority, it might "clarify" the question; it might "remove all doubt" about the sort of authority that the committee has. This sounds like a good thing to do. But how are we to understand Doar's answer? How can it be that "stating explicitly" is something that is essential to "fairness"? The conclusions reached by the committee could be fair or unfair; the way people are treated by the committee (the witnesses, the staff, the lawyers) could be fair or unfair. But how will the wording of the "preamble" of the resolution make something fair?

Some sort of answer to these questions must be attempted if I am going to have any success whatsoever in answering the question that I have set for myself, that is, what is good and bad about the talk about Watergate? One thing that should be clear already is that we have lawyer's talk. Recall that one of the first questions asked was about the scope of the investigation. Although that sort of query alone is not proof of the legal mind at work, the proposition that the scope of the investigation might be limited because of the resolutions of impeachment that had been previously filed does indeed seem to be a legal one. A nonlegalist might imagine that the resolutions gave a reason for having an investigation but should not define its scope. The second question that comes up is the power to issue subpoenas, and the colloquy is spoken in words that assume an understanding of law. Here we see the legal imagination at work, but not so much in what is said as in what Butler and Doar assume can go without saying. For example, if we look closely at Butler's questions, we find him assuming that any enlarging of the scope of the investigation would also enlarge the power to issue subpoenas; and so he wants to know whether the preamble is enlarging or merely clarifying the scope, and thus the power. The questions make sense only if we assume the existence of some legal rules about subpoenas, and assume that Butler and Doar know what they are.

But the most fascinating example of the legal imagination at work is the final assertion made by Doar: we must be explicit, and *not* because we want to enlarge our power, and *not even* to remove doubt about our power, but because an explicit statement will *make* what is happening into something that is *fair*. This sounds as though we are in a world in which legalized procedures are thought to be fair procedures, and they are fair because they are legalized. The circularity is puzzling.

What seems to be at stake here is some sort of doubt about the legitimacy of what the thirty-eight are setting out to do—by what right can such relative unknowns claim to judge a president? The text of the Constitution contains provisions about impeachment, but the procedure had been used only once against a president, and the standard history books do not describe the event as something to look back upon with pride. Consequently, the procedure has seemed, in modern times, more like a hypothetical possibility than a political possibility.

My own guess is that the proposal about the connection between explicitness and fairness is in fact talk about something else—that it is talk about authority and legitimacy. The underlying assertion seems to be something like this: "If we talk about this business in a lawyerlike way, we will have a symbolism that can give us a power and an authority that we might not otherwise have; we must remember that we are all politicians here; and by hypothesis, the president is a more successful politician than the rest of us; so we have to find a way of talking that will put the debate into a nonpolitical mode."

In other words, what is important about the law and legal language is the way in which it can support a claim of authority. If one is to act against a president, one must have authority to do so. Of course, the Constitution says that the House of Representatives can impeach executive officers such as the president, but the problem of political authority is more difficult. For the members of Congress, the more difficult question is how to transform the words of the document into political power that will be accepted by the public.

The claim to authority cannot be based upon personal merit; one cannot say, "I have the authority to judge the president because I am wise and honest." It may be true, and if true, it would be the best of reasons. But it wouldn't work. Perhaps it is something that we should be ashamed of, but it is true nonetheless: politicians cannot say that we should accept their claims to have authority because of their personal merit. Any such claim of superiority would sound too "aristocratic" for our democratic tastes.

In ordinary politics, one claims authority by claiming that one is representing the public interest, or if not the public interest, then some plausible part of it: a politician can purport to represent farmers, or workers, or business, and this kind of claim, if it appears to have some solid base, can be the source of power. But nothing of this sort seems plausible for the thirty-eight members of the House Judiciary Committee. They have a problem—how to convince the people to take them seriously—and the customary moves won't help.

If the ordinary moves of politics won't help, if the members of the Judiciary Committee cannot claim power by claiming to represent some politically powerful group such as business or labor, then they must find something else to represent. Their most plausible move is to try to represent an *idea*. If they can speak on behalf of an idea that we hold dear (national defense, health, the family), then they might have power.

What kind of ideas might one represent that would be powerful enough for impeaching a president? Honesty, democracy, the law, or what? If one looks back to the colloquy between John Doar and Caldwell Butler, it reads as though Doar believes that "explicitly" stating all of those things that lawyers can explicitly state will make what is done seem fair and therefore acceptable to the public. In short, the idea that he claims to represent is the idea of lawfulness.

Indeed, one can read the cautious legalisms with which the transcripts begin as dramatic gambits. Suppose that a zealous Nixon partisan was sneering at the way the proceedings were being organized, suggesting that this was nothing but a partisan lynching by the Democrats, who were merely trying to get revenge for having been humiliated by an overwhelming rejection at the polls. This sort of sneer must be refuted by deeds, not words; and we can perhaps feel the drama of seemingly dull words if we hear them as enacting the ritual of caution, if we see them as a performance that is meant to refute, by the very action itself, the charge of a precipitate rush to judgment.

If the performance is meant to refute by its deeds, let us contemplate what possible dramatic move might counter it. One might expect to see one of the moderate Republicans, not one of the zealots, step forward. Indeed, someone like Caldwell Butler, known for his keen mind and his integrity, might be the very sort of person who could test John Doar's ability to perform the ritual. And so there is some special drama in the fact that he is the first Republican to speak.

By reading in this way, we can emphasize the obvious facts that talk about Watergate was also argument about Watergate. The thirty-eight were not unanimous; they disagreed about some important things. Consequently, their talk was not an attempt to describe their consensus; they were trying to persuade—us, each other, and perhaps themselves. In persuading us, they had to convince us, and themselves, that what they said about Nixon was true, and they also needed to persuade us that they had the authority to say it. Judging from the way they started, their authority rested upon the law. However, saying this says very little. The law is not a single thing, nor is it a simple practice. We have criminal statutes and civil statutes; we have general principles of equity and we have specific rules for the taxation of income; we have constitutional law and ordinary law. It is essential to specify which part of the law will be important.

One alternative is to search for the narrowest possible legal grounds. For example, we could demand criminality. If we make this choice, then we are saying that a president may not be impeached unless he is a crook. I believe that our polity ought to have a higher moral tone than that, and I am pleased to report that our representatives also had higher ambitions for us than merely averting criminality. They went further and considered the broader constitutional question of the rule of law, and I believe that they were right to do so. However, they shrank back from going further still, and I hope to show that they were wrong in drawing the line where they drew it. As a first step in showing how they did draw the line, I would like to discuss Article III of the articles of impeachment, but before I proceed, let me summarize the foregoing.

My argument has been that if one looks beneath the surface of the opening debate, one sees that the committee members were struggling to establish their authority to proceed and that they were using the law as a way of gaining authority. There are, of course, some rather obvious objections to this argument. What I have said hardly adds up to a proof, since it is based upon too small a selection from the record; indeed, it looks as though I have made a mountain out of a molehill. Furthermore, there is a second objection. Not only is the evidence rather slim, but I have neglected to explore a plausible alternative hypothesis. Another way of explaining what is going on is to see it as mere puffery: they may have been using the language of the law, but as a false front; they may have been acting for other reasons. These are good criticisms, to which I have some partial answers.

It is certainly true that I have not constructed a proof; more evidence is needed. However, an argument must start somewhere; it is not possible to present all of the evidence at once. In the course of the book, I shall provide more evidence about the way in which the thirty-eight talked about Watergate. As for the question of sincerity versus hypocrisy, I think that this sort of question is oversimplified. People are complicated, and they generally act from mixed motives. Pure hypocrisy is rather rare. More important, these factual objections are aimed at the wrong fact. Even if their talk about law was meant to deceive us about their true reasons, why would they have tried to deceive us in this way? I have already argued that our representatives are experts in what can be safely said in public; perhaps in these debates they were saying what they thought we wanted to hear. In short, the factual questions are complicated. We cannot make simple dichotomies of sincerity versus hypocrisy; and even if we do, we have not disposed of the matter but merely raised a more elaborate question: why would a member of Congress think that legal talk would be politically advantageous?

However, I do not wish to defend my argument by quibbling about the facts. I want to ask how we should talk about Watergate. In answering this question, we can take advantage of the fact that there are those who have gone before us. The thirty-eight were compelled to answer the question, and they had to live with it for a long time. I wish to criticize what they said, but to do so, I must take them seriously. I hope that they spoke sincerely, but even if they didn't, I shall respond to what they said.

4 THE CENTRALLY STRATEGIC CHARGE

Article III poses the problem of power in the most naked sort of way. The committee was investigating, and so it needed evidence. The president had the evidence, and so members sent him a subpoena. He didn't comply. By definition, a subpoena is an order, and so a refusal to obey an order raises the question of authority, or power, in a rather fundamental way. The committee had to respond.

As noted, Article III passed by a small margin, only four votes (21–17). The first two articles passed by a sixteen-vote and an eighteen-vote margin (27–11, 28–10). One way to look at the voting on Article III is to see the closeness of the vote as evidence that the committee members had reached a difficulty of some especial seriousness. Consequently, this looks like the best place to start analyzing the votes.

McClory proposed the article of impeachment in which Nixon's refusal to obey the subpoena was declared to be an impeachable offense. You will recall that McClory was the only member of the Judiciary Committee who voted no on I but also voted yes on II and III, and this is one more reason to say that Article III is especially interesting. The theory of the article was that the committee had sought evidence that "was deemed necessary by the committee" for the proper conduct of its inquiry and that Nixon's refusal to honor the subpoena was "in derogation of the power of impeachment, vested solely in the House of Representatives by the Constitution of the United States."

In its rhetoric, Article III has the same form as do Articles I and II, and I would pause to examine that rhetoric. This examination will reveal that the articles are drafted broadly, so that the debate could potentially go in several different ways. In my judgment, those who drafted were correct in leaving matters open. It would have been wrong for the technical job of drafting to foreclose political debate.

In all three articles the beginning has a reference to the office; the phrase is "In his conduct of the office of President" or else it is "Using the powers of the office of President" (see Appendix). This language states a fact, but it also leaves open the possibility that this statement of fact implies a theory, which is that Nixon can be impeached only for official misconduct, not for private or personal misconduct. However, if this possibility is advanced, one would have to show how the line could be drawn, and this is not easy to do.

Immediately after this introductory flourish, the articles refer to the Constitution. When one examines the constitutional text, and identifies the provisions that relate to the president, one observes that most of the language is about the way in which the president is elected and about the powers of the office, but there is language in which duties appear to be imposed. For example, the Constitution prescribes an oath (or affirmation, should the president prefer to affirm rather than swear), and one can read this oath as containing two promises, and thus two duties: "I do solemnly swear (or affirm) that I will faithfully execute the Office of President of the United States and will to the best of my Ability, preserve, protect and defend the Constitution of the United States." The text also says that the President "shall take Care that the Laws be faithfully executed." There is other language that imposes duties, but these provisions are the most sweeping, and so the articles mention these three duties.

Of course, each of the powers granted to the president can be understood to be granted in trust, and consequently to be accompanied by a duty. For example, the Constitution states that the president "shall be Commander in Chief of the Army and Navy of the United States." I think that it is perfectly obvious that the president holds this power in trust and has a duty to use this power for the benefit of the public. Interestingly enough, the articles as drafted neither agree nor disagree with my interpretation. They do not specifically allege that every power is a trust, but they do allege that the president has a duty to live up to the oath by faithfully executing the office, and this language can be read as saying the same thing in different words. The matter is left open for argument.

After these opening flourishes, the articles proceed to the factual allegations: in Article I, the obstruction of justice; in Article II, the abuse of power; in Article III, the refusal to honor the subpoenas. In drafting these allegations, the drafters had to deal with the problem of specificity. No matter how precise a description might be, one can always make it more precise. For example, in Article III the subpoenas in question were identified by specifying the dates on which they were issued. It would have been possible to be more precise by quoting them verbatim. In the debate on Article I the issue of specificity was argued, but it was not a contested matter in the debate on Article III.

Then, having stated the duty, and having stated the facts that arguably constitute the breach of the duty, the articles end by asserting the conclusion: "In all of this, Richard M. Nixon has acted in a manner contrary to his trust as President and subversive of constitutional government, to the great prejudice of the cause of law and justice and to the manifest injury of the people of the United States." My own reading of this evaluation is that it asserts at least four grounds for impeachment: breach of trust, constitutionalism, rule of law, and injury to the people. In the debate any of these could be asserted, and each of them was.

Finally, the articles propose the action that should be taken: "Wherefore Richard M. Nixon, by such conduct, warrants impeachment and trial, and removal from office."

After McClory has introduced Article III, he begins by explaining what is at stake, and his first paragraphs are rather straightforward in their approach to the problem. He starts by noting that the Constitution gives the House the sole power to impeach, that the Judiciary Committee has been designated by the House to conduct an inquiry, and that if the recipient of a subpoena has the right to obey it or not, at will, then indeed the House does not have sole power of impeachment.

McClory's actual language is as follows:

In presenting this Article, Article III, it seems to me we are getting at something very basic and very fundamental insofar as our entire impeachment proceeding and inquiry is concerned. I think it is well for us to recall that the Constitution rests in us, the House of Representatives, and in us the House Judiciary Committee which has been designated by the House of Representatives to conduct this inquiry, with the sole power of impeachment. Now, implicit in that sole power of impeachment is the authority to make this inquiry, to investigate the office which is under investigation. In this case it happens to be the President of the United States. There have been a total, I believe, of thirteen impeachments in the House of Representatives, and a total of sixty-nine cases which have been referred and where there has been some action taken of one kind or another with regard to the subject of impeachment.

Now, implicit in this authority to conduct an impeachment inquiry is the authority to investigate the actions that take place in that office. If we are without that authority, or if the respondent has the right to determine for himself or herself to what extent the investigation shall be carried on, of course, we do not have the sole power of impeachment. Someone else is impinging upon our authority. So it seems to me implicit in this authority that we have a broad authority to conduct an investigative inquiry.

As a practical matter, it is hard to fault this statement: Of course, we could say that the members of the committee did not need any evidence; after all, the House of Representatives could vote to impeach without regard to the nature of the evidence, pro or con. But let us accept the judgment (and no one contested it) that the facts are relevant, and thus that any decision to impeach should be based on evidence. Given this judgment (we might call it a "value judgment"), the committee had to gather evidence. But who was to determine the scope of the investigation, Nixon or the members of the committee? The way one answers this question determines the allocation of power in the controversy.

As I read McClory's remarks, I find myself nodding yes, and perhaps other readers responded in the same way. But why are we agreeing? Perhaps we are interpreting the text of the constitution, and we agree with McClory's interpretation. The text says that the House is to have "the sole power," and so if the committee, in acting for the House, must share its decisions with Richard Nixon, and thus let him jointly determine the scope of its investigation, then the committee's power to investigate is not "sole" but "joint." Or perhaps that is not what impresses us; perhaps we are not really convinced by the linguistics of the word "sole." Instead, we might be moved by the pragmatic and commonsense tone of his words. McClory makes a straightforward means-end argument: the House has the power to impeach, and the power to subpoena is a means to that end. Of course, we need not choose between judging on the basis of the ancient text versus judging on the basis of practical necessities; in this example, they march together.

Let us return to the argument and consider what more can be said, pro or con. McClory has stated the issue and given a short, simple, and cogent argument for his position; should he now sit down? Of course, he doesn't; he has more to say. I think we can understand why there is more to say, why any of us, were we in his position, would want to say more. Impeaching a president is not an ordinary sort of thing. Whenever extraordinary things have to be done, we feel some sort of responsibility to justify our actions. This sort of reaction—the need to accompany action with speech—is something that most of us share; and politicians probably feel it even more strongly than we are likely to do.

What, then, does McClory say? Having stated the issue, he next talks about how the committee has tried to be cooperative and thus negotiate with the president before issuing subpoenas; and he states that the committee members have tried to act in a nonpartisan way. Not only have they been cooperative and bipartisan, but they were willing to make special arrangements about confidentiality. They offered to receive the subpoenaed material under rules of strict confidentiality; furthermore, they also offered to let the president or his counsel join with the counsel for the committee in screening out national security information. However, the president insisted upon being the "sole arbiter."

These comments are meant, I am sure, to persuade us that the committee was justified in issuing the subpoenas, and thus that Nixon was wrong in not honoring them. Let us ask, then, whether we are persuaded, and if so, why we are. I understand McClory as saying that the committee has been judicious, acting reasonably, calmly giving each side its due. The notion would be that its task is partly judicial, and thus that judicious conduct was appropriate. Our agreement might be based on an assent to judiciousness as the proper norm.

However, McClory could also be acknowledging the norms of cooperation as purely political norms. Compromise is one of the key norms of our political life. Although it is true that representatives are elected to represent different sorts of interests, and thus it is also true that we expect to find some radical differences in political views among them, even so there is still a need for compromise. If on every issue, every member were to hold out, insisting on adhering to individual preferences, then nothing could get done. I can understand and assent to this view of legislative politics.

Even if this description is accurate, it is puzzling to understand exactly why these comments about bipartisanship and cooperation are a critique of Nixon. McClory is saying that the committee has acted properly by being bipartisan and cooperative and that Nixon has violated these basic norms of politics. When McClory makes this argument, he is necessarily assuming that his audience knows what needs to be known. The members of the committee are all politicians, and they are presumably experts in the rules of the game. In particular, they should be expert about what has to be done to keep things moving along. Our system of governing ourselves is complex; we have a scheme known as separation of powers, by which power is dispersed and thus shared among different political actors.

Given this complex scheme, we could have here an allusion to what the insiders know about how this scheme really works, and also about what politicians have to do to keep it working. We obviously have a great deal of room for confrontation and partisanship in our system, but in his hour of need, McClory begins his persuasion (after he has opened by clarifying what the issue is) by trying to persuade us that the committee has been cooperative and that the president has been uncooperative. We wonder, then, if we should read between the lines and say that Nixon should be impeached because he violated one of the norms about how power should be shared.

If we are persuaded by this sort of argument, we will have made a set of commitments that are different from those called forth by the previous argument. That previous argument was linked to the assertion of a textually based power. The power was derived from the text in two ways: directly, by way of interpreting the word "sole"; and indirectly, by way of implying a means to execute the textual power of "impeachment." The argument from the norm of cooperation is extratextual. The claim is that there is a practice—that is, that we have developed customs about the way in which those in government should go about exercising the powers that they hold—and the further claim is that these customs have normative power, such that one who violates them has done something wrong. Should we agree to the argument from custom? At times we have relied upon customs, and our reliance does give rise to expectations that we regard as reasonable and that should be protected. But then we must be ready to defend against the charge that these customs are too indefinite to provide a solid ground for judgment, and we must be prepared to meet an even more radical attack, which is that an extratextual custom should never bind us.

Next McClory turns to another theme. He points out that the president has been involved in litigation with the special prosecutor on the question of executive privilege. His interpretation of the outcome of that litigation is that "the doctrine of absolute executive privilege has fallen." Such a doctrine has even less of a place in impeachment proceedings because of "the maxim enunciated by Lord Coke that a person cannot be the judge of his own cause." Furthermore, McClory says that the committee needs "to set a standard and a guide for future Congresses," and so it is important not to let its authority be destroyed.

These remarks can be read as a turn to "the legal." McClory takes as the source of his norms a contemporary decision of the U.S. Supreme Court and the opinion in Calvin's case by Lord Coke, the distinguished seventeenth-century English jurist. He is not finding norms in what he knows about the daily practice of his colleagues; he is drawing upon what he can read in Coke's *Reports* and the *U.S. Reports*. And furthermore, one of the arguments for doing something is that it would set a good precedent.

McClory next turns to future consequences. He claims that "if we are going to set a standard and a guide for future Congresses," then Article III must be passed. The reason is simple enough: "The future respondents will be in a position where they can determine themselves what they are going to provide in an impeachment inquiry and what they are not going to provide." This can be read as a concern for precedent in the narrow sense, and it can also be read more broadly as concerned with power, with the credibility of a claim for power:

Now, I say this is fundamental and basic to our inquiry and I mean precisely that. I mean that if we are going to set a standard and a guide for future Congresses, for future impeachment inquiries, there is no more important standard and guide than the one that we will determine with respect to Article III, because if we refuse to recommend impeachment of the President on the basis of this Article III, if we refuse to recommend that the President should be impeached because of his defiance of the Congress with respect to the subpenas [sic] that we have issued, the future respondents will be in the position where they can determine themselves what they are going to provide in an impeachment inquiry and what they are not going to provide, and this would be particularly so in the case of an inquiry directed toward the President of the United States.

So, it not only affects this President but future Presidents. And it might be that a Republican Congress would be investigating in an impeachment inquiry a Democratic President in a future instance. I hope we do not have any more impeachments, but in the case we did, the precedent that we might establish here would be effective then.

So, it seems to me that there is no greater responsibility which befalls us at this time than that to determine this question of the President's responsibility with respect to our subpenas [sic].

To this part of McClory's speech, as to others, we might nod our assent, but we would be assenting to a complicated argument. He is saying that we should care about the sort of precedent that our actions will establish. Caring about the future, caring about the possible consequences if present acts are taken as precedents in the future, is probably a good idea. There are some simple prudential reasons for this kind of looking forward. In politics, for example, one makes promises and threats and then acts on them. To be politically effective, words must have some credibility, and they won't have any unless they are backed up by action. In this context, it is easy to understand McClory's argument that power for the future can be lost by a failure to exercise power in the present.

In the last two paragraphs of McClory's opening remarks, he offers his conclusion and states some things that one does not ordinarily hear. We should attend carefully:

Now, earlier I had the thought and I set it forth publicly that I felt that when the President did not respond to our subpenas that we should take action to hold the President in contempt, or that we should censure the President, or we should have a resolution of inquiry, to get some action on the part of the House. I was discouraged in that respect. I was discouraged from leaders on both sides of the aisle, I might say, and I emphasized at that time that while I was withholding the action that I intended to take then, that I would face a very serious dilemma at this stage, and so while we did not take action under the contempt authority that we had, which in a sense is quite difficult to enforce and to apply.

Nevertheless we are now faced with this decision at this hour of decision, with determining whether or not the President is or is not in contempt of Congress, and if he is whether he has denied the Congress to the extent that we should recommend his impeachment. I think that this is an important Article. It is a case where the Congress itself is pitted against the Executive. We have this challenge on the part of the Executive with respect to our authority, and if we think of the whole process of impeachment, let us recognize that this is a power which is preeminent, which makes the Congress of the United States dominant with respect to the three separate and co-equal branches of government. It bridges the separation of powers and gives us and reposes in us the responsibility to fulfill this mission. And the only way we can do it is through acting favorably on Article III.

Speaking only for myself, I find McClory's performance to be remarkable. He is versatile in drawing upon a variety of norms (from judicial practice, from legislative practice, from interbranch practice), and he is skillful in weaving them together. Moreover, he does not let this multiplicity of norms diffuse the focus of his argument; he begins and ends with the basic question of power, and he uses his several arguments in as many ways to justify a single position.

However, although he won the vote, he lost the argument. Thornton proposed an amendment to Article III that changed its spirit; the amendment carried; the Article III that ultimately passed was the amended version. And so in some way McClory's views were not representative. Even before you read on, you might, perhaps, be able to guess why. He posed the question as being an ultimate question of power. When our representatives pull back from that position, perhaps we can see ourselves in the shrinking back. Perhaps most of us would have tried to find some narrower grounds. We do not have the reputation, as a people, of attending to ultimate questions. As individuals we might regard ourselves as men and women of principle, but we as a people are devoted to the pragmatics of compromise.

On a first reading of the Thornton amendment, it is not at all obvious what the whys and wherefores of it are, since it can be read as a minor technical change. In McClory's draft, there was a sentence that might have struck most readers as innocuous because innocuously descriptive: "The subpoenaed papers and things were deemed necessary by the committee to its inquiry." However, this sentence must not have been innocuous, for Thornton offered an elaborate substitute (note the phrase "other evidence"): "The subpoenaed papers and things were deemed necessary by the committee" (so far, no change, but next is the new language) "in order to resolve *by direct evidence* fundamental, factual questions relating to Presidential direction, knowledge or approval of actions *demonstrated by other evidence* to be substantial grounds for impeachment of the President" (emphasis added).

The logic of these changes is simple enough, although it doesn't jump out on first reading. McClory's draft stated that the committee had made a judgment that the subpoena was necessary, but it did not say why it was necessary. Thornton's draft stated a particular grounds of necessity: the tapes and papers that were subpoenaed would resolve questions raised by other evidence that was already in the record.

We wonder why Thornton would think this change important. When we look at the transcript we see that as he begins to speak, he does not start with this detail, but with broader grounds: although refusal to comply with the subpoenas is indeed an impeachable offense, it should have been made part of Article I or II, since the refusal was part of the pattern of obstruction of justice and abuse of power that was alleged in those articles. In other words, Thornton argues that a refusal to honor subpoenas, standing alone, is not enough, although the refusal in this particular context is impeachable.

The next step in the argument is to establish that Article III is needed. Its necessity is established by way of colloquy with counsel about the admissibility of evidence in a trial in the Senate. In the colloquy Thornton and counsel agree on two things: as Articles I and II are drafted, Nixon's refusal to comply with the subpoenas can be admitted in evidence as relevant to a previous charge that he had interfered with congressional investigations of the Watergate burglary and its cover-up; but counsel cannot argue that the failure to respond to the subpoena is an independent grounds for finding an impeachable offense.

With these technicalities in place, Thornton states his problem, which he puts by way of a dilemma. On the one hand, doing nothing could "limit [our] authority . . . to make a proper inquiry." On the other hand, asserting too broad a power in impeachment "might distort the balance of power." In other words, Thornton agrees with McClory that Article III raises a fundamental question, but he wants to shy away from it.

Thornton's argument is as follows:

I think that it is important that in approaching this we should be aware that here we are dealing with directly and intimately a matter which can have a bearing upon the constitutional basis of power between the three departments of government, and that what we may do with regard to the adoption of this Article is going to in one way or another possibly affect the future of those balances.

If we do nothing, we may indeed limit the authority of the legislative branch to make a proper inquiry as to the misconduct under the impeachment provision of individuals in either the executive or judicial branches of government. If, on the other hand we draw too broadly upon our power and authority, we might distort the balance of power to give the legislative branch under its impeachment clause the authority to constitutionally investigate and determine the actions of members of the executive or judicial branches of government.

For this reason it seems to me that if this Article is to be given consideration, it must be sharply limited and defined to the presence of offenses established by the other evidence which might rise to the level of impeachable offenses. And that is the purpose and effect of the perfecting amendment which I have offered and which I ask the members to adopt, because it seems to me that we are confronted with the very serious problem in Presidential noncompliance with our subpenas, but that we must draw carefully limiting language to prevent a distortion of the balance of power between the executive and legislative branch.

Thornton's proposal is analogous to a procedural device that we use in criminal procedure: the "probable cause" requirement. Before a search warrant is issued, the police officers must present to the magistrate an affidavit that establishes probable cause. For example, if there is to be a search for stolen goods, the affidavit must present some good reason for believing that the goods are in the place where the officer wants to search for them. In its present form, this requirement is a compromise: the judges don't want to let the police search whenever they might want to search, but then they don't want to cut off searches absolutely; the procedural solution of probable cause is a middle ground.

Why should we believe that this solution, which doesn't work too well in criminal law, will work in impeachment? And more generally, why believe that any legal technicality can solve the problem of maintaining a proper balance of power between the Congress and the president?

I have set out what McClory and Thornton said at some length, but I would now like to proceed rather more briskly. While it is good to know the details, and while it seemed an especially good idea to set out the details of what was said by such crucial "swing men" as McClory and Thornton, even so I think that we must not get lost in the details: the most important thing is to have some sort of feel for the way the details of the argument fit together. In other words, what any one person said is not important, if we pull it out of the debate and look at it in isolation; what is important is the way what was said fits together in the ebb and flow of a debate; what is important is the overall pattern of the debate, for the overall pattern is what shaped the issues and set the terms on which the thirty-eight talked about Watergate.

However, if one picks up the transcript for the first time, intending to read it so as to find a pattern, one will not find any pattern on that first reading. This is not evidence that there is no pattern, but it is true that there is a problem in seeing it. The source of the problem is understandable, and experience that most of us share can help in understanding it. Most of us have participated in meetings at which a large number of people got up and spoke. One knows how such meetings go: the first speaker starts it off; the second speaker is likely to introduce a completely new topic; the third speaker may respond to something that was said before the meeting got started; the fourth speaker responds to what the first speaker said; the fifth responds to a newspaper editorial; the sixth then responds to the second; and so forth. There is a pattern to be found in meetings like these, and an agenda is established, but one cannot find it by limiting oneself to the strict chronology of what was said.

Consequently, I shall reconstruct the debate, by taking arguments from here and there in the transcript and reordering them. There is no particular magic to the particular reordering that I have chosen, but I do hope that it will make reasonably clear how the debate went. In due course I shall quote more extensively the exact rhetoric that was used. However, I wish to begin as I have suggested, in order to bring out the overall shape of the debate. Of course, the members of the committee had no problem in understanding the shape of the debate: they were right there in the middle of it; they had been together for six months; and so they were able to keep several different arguments going at one time. My reconstruction, however, does not assume such familiarity.

Needless to say, I shall not be quoting exactly, for I shall have to reword what was said so as to make it fit in the new context. What follows is the spirit and not the letter of the debate.

The debate goes something like this, beginning with a defender of the president, then picking up something from the other side, and so back and forth.

—The Supreme Court has now recognized the existence of an executive privilege and has further said that it is not an absolute privilege. The president has claimed, as against us, a privilege. It is wrong to impeach him for claiming a privilege without going to court and testing the legitimacy of his claim.

—But the claim, on the merits, is ridiculous. It fell in that case in a criminal prosecution; impeachment is surely more important, and it is even more clear that it falls here.

—Well, if it's so clear, why don't you go to court? It must not be all that clear, or you wouldn't be afraid to go to court.

—I'll tell you why we shouldn't go to court. The Constitution says that we have the sole power of impeachment, and it follows that we have jurisdiction to decide this question. We have no more right to refuse a jurisdiction which is ours than we have to assume a jurisdiction that is not ours.

—But what is the scope of our jurisdiction? That is a constitutional question on which the judiciary has the final say, not Congress. And furthermore, in exercising our jurisdiction, we don't have the right to destroy anyone's privileges.

—I'm sorry, but I don't see how any of this helps Nixon. If he wants to go to court, he can go to court and make a motion to quash the subpoena. You know as well as I do that that's the law of subpoenas.

—Without regard to these technicalities, I have a more substantial defense. The theory behind this article is illogical in that what you are saying today is completely inconsistent with what you said yesterday. Only yesterday, I told you that you didn't have enough evidence to support Articles I and II, but you told me then that you did. Now, today, you come in here and say that the president is holding back some evidence that you need to resolve some fundamental questions in the facts. You are being illogically inconsistent.

—Wait a minute; that's wrong. You are looking at this too narrowly. By law, we are entitled to all of the relevant evidence; we are not limited to that which is merely sufficient to support the charges.

—But it's just not fair. You're saying that a bare majority of this committee could tell the president to open his files and then treat a partial compliance as an impeachable offense. This would destroy separation of powers.

—There isn't any separation-of-powers problem with this article; we have three branches of government, not three governments.

—True, but no branch is supposed to give orders to any other branch. Think about our own privileges.

—Those privileges are written into the Constitution so as to make us strong against the executive. All branches are equal, but some are more equal than others.

—There's too much talk about power, and not enough about common sense. This Article III is overkill. Articles I and II are enough to get the case before the Senate so as to subject the president's conduct to trial; any additional articles would extend the proceedings unnecessarily. Enough is enough; let's get away from these broad questions of power.

—That is a good argument against the original draft, but as amended, Article III is far more narrow. As amended, there must be a nexus between the evidence sought and what has been shown by other evidence.

—Perhaps, but I fear that this so-called nexus between the subpoenaed evidence and the other evidence is more fictional than real. Did we ever in fact make the preliminary findings of the sort that this article claims were made? I do not believe that we imposed any such procedure on ourselves.

Let me expand my summary now by offering some of the actual arguments. Consider the question of consistency. Wiggins of California made the following argument:

Mr Chairman, I rise in opposition to the amendment. The maker of the main position, you see, has dug himself a hole and the purpose of the amendment is to help extricate himself from that illogical position. The situation is this. This committee yesterday and the day before viewed the evidence and found it, I am told, overwhelming. I believe our good counsel called it a surfeit of evidence. I take that to be a good bit, Mr. Doar. And voted to impeach and remove the President based thereon, found it to be clear and convincing.

And now we seek to impeach him because he did not give us enough evidence to do the job. . . .

Now, if logic and common sense still has any place to play in these proceedings, I would think that we had an election. We elect to impeach on the basis of the evidence before us or we elect to impeach him for failing to provide that evidence. Those who voted for the first two articles cannot have their cake and eat it, too, and maintain logical consistency by voting for the third, in my opinion. In my opinion, this article is inconsistent with the prior two.

Seiberling responded as follows:

I am a bit surprised by the argument of the gentleman from California, Mr. Wiggins. Mr. Wiggins is a very, very able lawyer, and he knows in a court trial you are entitled, the parties are entitled, to all of the relevant evidence, not enough or barely sufficient to support a particular point of view, but all of the evidence because the more evidence you can get the stronger your case is and the better chance you have of prevailing. That is an argument which I think is so easily disposed of by any lawyer practicing in the courts that I am surprised that he would even make it.

These two excerpts give one a feel for the skill that could be displayed in these debates. The debates were sharp, but they were not always solemn. Consider the following rather folksy argument offered by Hungate:

I support this article and feel more strongly about it than any other. I respect those who disagree, and as I hear the arguments I think I know why there are no law suits in heaven. The other side has all of the good lawyers. . . .

But, how are we to obtain evidence? We got it in this case by accident.

When you talk of the separation of powers and the confrontation we face here, I am indebted to another fine Congressman, the late George Andrews from Alabama for my education on this subject that deeply impressed me, that we do have three co-equal branches. But as Speaker McCormack used to say, "All members of the Congress are equal, but some are more equal than others." I think all branches of government are equal, but some are more equal. You can become President without being elected. We have had some tragic assassinations. Lyndon B. Johnson and Andrew Johnson both became President without being elected. In fact, Andrew was never elected. You can go to the Senate without being elected. Members serve there and they are never elected, they go back and they are simply appointed.

But, you cannot come in the House of Representatives without passing before the people and being elected. And you only serve for two years. You had better be close to the people, you had better refresh your "mandate." This is the reason why I think the Founding Fathers put the sole power of impeachment in the Congress, the power to impeach the President in the Congress, the power to impeach the Supreme Court Justices in the Congress, and the ultimate power in the case of confrontation in the body nearest to the people, closest to the people's control. I submit the House of Representatives is that body, and I cannot acquiesce in agreeing that it is an inferior body, or in making it one now. If we are to simply push papers, there are many paper pushers of independence who will choose to do that elsewhere.

However, several members who were in the middle block of swing voters fell away on this article. I think it is worth quoting at least two of them. First, consider Butler's argument:

Whether the House of Representatives shall impeach or not is in many ways a matter of discretion. We have a great deal of discretion as to whether or not we will impeach, and within the framework of our decision as to whether an impeachable offense exists or not, there is still the judgment which is reposed in us to determine whether it is in the best interests of the country to impeach or not to impeach under those circumstances.

In my judgment we will have placed after adoption of Articles I and II by the House of Representatives, we will have placed the issue of Presidential conduct sufficiently before the Senate of the United States for a determination of whether the President should be continued in the office or not. And any additional articles would extend the proceedings unnecessarily. We do not need this article, and it serves no useful purpose to pursue it, and I would recommend against it.

The principal problem for me with reference to this article is whether the conduct standing alone is an impeachable offense under the Constitution. I think not. I am concerned, however, that what we do in substance by Article III is to impeach a President for a failure to cooperate in his own impeachment, and to me that is basically unfair. In my judgment the House of Representatives has a responsibility to go further down the road than we have at this moment before we impeach the president for his noncompliance with our subpenas.

I would prefer that our determination be affirmed by the courts in an appropriate proceeding, or at least by a preliminary determination of a contempt in an appropriate proceeding before the House.

The issue is also one of legislative responsibility. We are saying today, if we pass Article III, that twenty members, a bare majority of the thirty-eight member committee, can, for reasons deemed as sufficient unto themselves, issue a subpena to the President and recommend his impeachment for their judgment as to the sufficiency of his partial compliance with the subpena. This article offends my sense of fair play, and I intend to vote against it.

Flowers was also opposed. He spoke as follows:

Mr. Chairman and colleagues, I have voted for two articles of impeachment here because I was clearly convinced that they should have been supported, and the evidence and the facts justified each, although I had a great deal of reluctance. Now, here in this instance I am just as clearly convinced, and I do not have any reluctance whatsoever in voting against article III. And I seriously, seriously ask that my friends on this side and the two lonesome ones on the other side that appear to be voting for it, and it is kind of lonesome over here on this side, opposing it, I ask that you consider what we are doing here.

And let us not kid ourselves. If this article were standing alone, and I think that is the way we must look at it, but if it were standing alone, would we be seriously thinking about impeaching the President of the United States for this charge?

Now, there may be some that disagree with me, but I honestly think not for the majority of this committee, and I do not see how we can possibly approach it in any other way. Perhaps we are too imbued with our new found power. We have been thinking too much about the House having the sole power of impeachment. I do not know what it is that brings us to this point. But this is going too far for me, and I cannot consider impeaching the President of the United States for this charge. It is just not sufficient.

Now, here are the kind of things that run through my mind, and again this is me. At some point, at least for me, there is a question of whether the President must comply with a subpena issued by this committee. I think that at some point that the President, the Chief Executive, has an opportunity to raise the issue of whether or not he has already given enough evidence. I certainly do not think we are anywhere near approaching it in this instance, but we did not take the necessary steps to elevate this to the status of an impeachable offense.

Second then, we could have elevated this to the level of an impeachable offense by either going to the House floor or going to the Courts, as my colleague from Illinois, Mr. Railsback, suggested. In this particular, you might argue that we are putting the cart before the horse.

I think as my colleague from Arkansas has suggested, it would be better placed in either Article I or Article II that we have already voted on. I would probably oppose it as an inclusion, but it would certainly more than likely be acceptable to most in one of those articles.

Stepping back from the dialectic of these arguments, what do they add up to? To me, what seems most remarkable in their rich variety. The arguments range from narrow appeals to technicalities of the law of subpoenas to the grand theoretics of separation of powers; there are appeals to logical consistency and to prudential discretion. Given this diversity, the question is: over the course of the rest of the votes, which of these arguments seem decisive?

We can't judge too well from this article alone. It is true that Thornton's amendment was adopted, and this is evidence that the members were nervous about taking the broadest view of the matter. And it is also true that Thornton's technique for narrowing Mc-Clory's draft is a legal technique, and thus we see here the legal imagination at work. Even so, we can't draw too many conclusions.

Even if the legal imagination is at work, we can't yet say very much about the positive shape of that imagination. For example, there is no reason to say that the members of the committee are taking a narrowly legalistic view of the matter. Some of them seem more legalistic than others, but most of the thirty-eight seem to have a realistic understanding of the limits of the law. They do not imagine that there are rules written down in lawbooks that have already solved all of their problems. They do not talk as though they saw it as their only task to find some rules and then make a straightforward application of the rules to the facts. They understand that they have to make some difficult judgments and that there is nothing in the books that will ease their burden.

However, even though they do not imagine that words in lawbooks can solve all of their problems, it is also true that law is very important to them. Their debate is filled with legal talk, and so my own best judgment about how to characterize their talk goes something like this: they use legal metaphors to address the problem, and yet they also know that the problem is more than legal. Perhaps I can state the matter another way, using the logician's categories of "necessary" and "sufficient": they talk as though the use of law is a necessary part of making their judgments, but not sufficient for the making of them.

Even so, I am disturbed; even if I give the committee members the benefit of a charitable reading, it is still true that they pulled back from giving a broad interpretation to their own power. A broad interpretation could rest upon a politically plausible, and historically justified, interpretation of the Constitution. The House of Representatives is supposed to be the most representative, and thus the most democratic, of the national political institutions. Furthermore, one could argue—as Hungate did—that this theory of the House as democratic is relevant to impeachment. One could argue that the House of Representatives should be the tribune of the people and that its power to impeach is its most important power for holding the executive accountable to the people. As I read the debates, this theory of democratic accountability was offered in support of Article III, but the Thornton amendment, which passed, seems to reject this theory. Consequently, our representatives did not seem most interested in strengthening democracy, and thus they would not describe the Watergate affair as a threat to democracy, but as involving something else.

5 A CRUCIAL NEGATIVE VOTE

In investigating how all of the arguments go together, the negative votes are more valuable than the positive votes. This might sound bizarre, but it isn't. The negative votes can help us understand the committee members' words in a way that is analogous to our use of "exceptions" to aid in our understanding of "rules." One of the best ways to grasp the scope of a rule is to examine its exceptions, that is, the way in which it is not used. Hence the well-known maxim: the exception proves (tests) the rule. The advice that is inherent in this ancient maxim is relevant to understanding the votes on impeachment. The trouble with reading the arguments in support of the positive votes is that the positive votes were accompanied by a host of words in which we can find many different reasons for impeaching Nixon; to put it more strongly, we find too many reasons, and so it is hard to know which ones were most persuasive. But the negative votes give us a way to check these multiple arguments and sort out the ones that seem most important. For example, if an argument justifies a yes vote on Article I but would also require a yes vote on V, and if the person who makes the argument votes yes on I but no on V, then we don't have to worry about that argument. Of course, the case that I have just proposed by way of an example does not occur in the pure form. Instead, we get arguments that can be interpreted in several different ways, and then the no votes let us select which interpretations are most plausible.

In the last article, the charge was that Nixon had used the powers of his office to enrich himself. We call this sort of thing corruption, and in the United States it is a classic charge in politics. In Nixon's case, one of the two allegations was that he had acted so as to increase the compensation due him in a manner that was unlawful: it was charged that he had government money spent to improve his property at San Clemente and Key Biscayne. The other allegation was that he was guilty of tax fraud: it was said that he had deliberately underpaid his taxes by misstating his income; he did not report more than three-quarters of a million dollars of income from 1969 to 1972.

In interpreting the debate on the tax-fraud article, one must bear in mind that it came on the last day of the debates, the evening of the sixth day. The debate opened on Wednesday, July 24, 1974, at 7:45 P.M. During that evening of the first day and during an afternoon and evening session of the second day, the members made their opening statements. On the third and fourth days, Friday and Saturday, the members debated Article I. They took a break on Sunday, and then Monday the twenty-ninth was devoted to Article II. Tuesday was the sixth day, and the final votes on the last three articles were taken on that day. I emphasize this chronology, for one can base several inferences upon it. One is that the committee members were tired and ready to quit; I think this is a fair inference. However, it is not obvious what the next conclusions should be. Does one infer from their being tired that they spoke carelessly? I think not. My own deduction is that by this point they all knew what all of the arguments were, there was no need to say much, and thus being tired merely encouraged a brevity that was otherwise appropriate. At any rate, the debate was brief. The transcript for the entire six days comprises 560 printed pages; the debate on Article V is in the last 43.

The speakers debated the income tax fraud, and they did not talk much about the illegal compensation. We can sympathize with their obsessions, for the word "taxes" is a dangerous word for politicians; to say it aloud can be a risky thing to do, and so they turn to it in the way that one gazes at a sore, a boil.

How should this question be argued? There are technicalities of tax law, and there are questions of evidence. For example, a key item in the tax-fraud part of this article was a charitable deduction of over a half million dollars that Nixon claimed for giving papers to the United States. By law, the cutoff date for the validity of such gifts was July 25, 1969. A mass of papers were delivered before this date, but there was no intent to make a gift of all the papers delivered; instead, the actual papers that were to be the gift were to have been chosen sometime later. As it turns out, the selection occurred after the cutoff date. Then a deed was signed on April 10, 1970 (about nine months after the cutoff date), but the deed was backdated so as to make it appear that it had been signed a year earlier, on April 21, 1969. This was clearly an illegal act, but there are some evidentiary problems. The backdated deed was signed not by Nixon himself, but by someone who purported to be acting on his behalf; further, this purported agent did not have any written authority. It is not clear whether Nixon knew what was happening, or whether the agent acted with his approval.

The direct evidence of Nixon's involvement is rather minimal. In 1968, when it was legal, Nixon gave some of his papers to the archives and took a charitable deduction on his income tax form. In 1969 Ehrlichman sent a memo to Nixon recommending that he give some more papers to the archives; Nixon agreed. However, while his subordinates were working on this recommendation, a tax-reform bill was going through Congress (a bill that Nixon signed into law), and this bill disallowed such deductions. The only other fact that is solidly nailed down is that on April 10, 1970, Frank De Marco and Herbert Kalmbach, lawyers from Los Angeles, went into the Oval Office of the White House carrying a completed tax return for 1969; they were in the office for no more than thirty-five minutes, and probably less than half of that time was spent going over the return. The lawyers have testified that they told Nixon that the deduction was proper.

This is not much evidence on the crucial question concerning the extent of Nixon's involvement. There is some circumstantial evidence from which one might draw an inference. (And that is lawyer's jargon for saying: the situation stinks.) The amount of money involved is so large that one would expect him to be interested in and knowledgeable about what was happening. This inference is strengthened by the fact that Nixon, as a habitual matter, gave a close, personal scrutiny to his own financial affairs and was intimately involved in transactions that were far smaller. Thus the inference from general human nature is helped along by what we know of his own character and his conduct in analogous situations.

Finally, we have some acts after the fact that can be used to infer what happened before the fact: Nixon refused to cooperate in the investigation. Lawyers and investigators for the IRS and the congressional Joint Committee on Internal Revenue Taxation tried to get more information, but the witnesses were not cooperative. The joint committee sent Nixon some written questions, but he refused to answer them. The commissioner of the IRS wrote a letter to the special prosecutor (by this time it was Jaworski, who had succeeded Cox) in which he said that the IRS was unable to do a complete investigation and in which he recommended that the grand jury go into the question of tax fraud.

My own opinion is that what these things add up to as a matter of proof turns on what sort of standard of proof you care to employ. Certainly they do not constitute "proof beyond a reasonable doubt" as we use that phrase in criminal law, and they may not be "clear and convincing," which is the standard that the members of the committee said they were going to use. But it is also reasonably obvious that the failure of proof is Richard Nixon's fault. And once I reach this conclusion, I am struck by the fact that in Article III, the committee declared that Nixon's noncooperation was an impeachable offense. Why didn't it do something similar here?

Consequently, I am inclined to discount the uncertainty in the evidence. Although several members of the committee said that the lack of evidence was a reason for voting no, there were others who believed that there was something wrong with the charge itself. Perhaps tax fraud should not be an impeachable offense. If we read the arguments, it turns out that there were many who thought it should not.

Mezvinsky led the argument for the proponents of Article V. First he summarized the evidence and stated what he thought that it proved. After he finished arguing the evidence, he moved to the arguments about principles. At this point he could have woven eloquent rhetoric about how shameful it is not to pay one's taxes; but he didn't. Instead he anticipated the defense that others could make, which was the defense that this was not "official conduct." He said: "I think we are all aware that some have argued, and this is a key point in our debate, that a President can be impeached only for criminal conduct, and then there are others who contend that this tax matter, although involving criminal conduct, is not an impeachable offense because it involves 'unofficial conduct.' "

Mezvinsky, at this point, could have called those who take such positions stupid, or corrupt, but to charge a lack of intellectual capacity or moral integrity in one's opponent is to end the argument, not continue it. If Mezvinsky was to make an argument, as distinguished from ending it, there were two sorts of moves that he could make: he could try to persuade his opponents that they had adopted the wrong set of premises; or he could try to persuade them that they were reaching the wrong result from the right premises. Had he adopted the former strategy, he would have needed to argue that any violation of a criminal statute, if the offense was serious, was an impeachable offense. However, Mezvinsky did not take this approach. Instead, he met his opponents on their own ground. He conceded that the mere signing of the tax return was not an official act, but then he argued that if Nixon had not been president, he would have been prosecuted for tax evasion; the official act was taking advantage of the presidency.

Mezvinsky's actual words are as follows:

Now, I think we should take a look at the President's conduct and see whether or not it is impeachable. All of us on the committee know that if one of us took an unlawful deduction for a half million dollars on our tax returns, we would be subject to criminal prosecution. The President's signing of his tax returns may not be an official act but it is likely that if it weren't for his official capacity, he, too, would be prosecuted for willful tax evasion.

But unfortunately, due to his special position, really only the impeachment process can call the President into account for his actions.

We must also confront this evidence as an extension of the abuse of IRS. Last night we heard members—Walter Flowers, Alabama; Tom Railsback, from Illinois—speak so eloquently about the abuse of IRS and how it corrodes the system.

Well, let me say that I think this falls in that category because we have a President who, due to his position, could assume that his tax returns were not subject to the same scrutiny as those of other taxpayers. Rather than taking care to insure that his tax returns complied with the laws, he took advantage of the Presidency to avoid paying his proper tax.

And really what is more significant, and this to me is the key, is that this poses a serious threat to our tax system which operates on the premise that everyone is expected to be honest. The reason it works so well is that we expect the laws to be equally applied to every taxpayer, whether he is a resident of Iowa or Alabama, Massachusetts, New Jersey, Arkansas or whether he resides in the White House.

And when the President of these United States refuses to be bound by the revenue laws and if he escapes the judgment here as he evaded his taxes, then it is not just the treasury that is poorer. The very integrity of our system of self-government is diminished.

The overall structure of the argument that follows, and here I paraphrase, goes something like this (once again, I start with a defender).

—In impeachment, we deal with official acts that damage our system of government, but there is nothing official about signing a tax return.

—Not for you and me, perhaps; but he's the president.

—You can't be serious; we can't go after every personal misdeed of the man.

—But this one is special. The tax system depends upon voluntary self-assessment, and the president ought to set an example.

—Now look, he's paid his back taxes, with interest; and he is not a wealthier man now than he was when he took office.

—If he had been an ordinary citizen, he would have been prosecuted. This involves more than not paying taxes; it involves abuse of power.

—The matter has gone to the special prosecutor; why isn't that remedy enough? We have some discretion. Let's not load up the case too much.

—We are the only tribunal that can hold the president accountable; we must meet our responsibilities.

—But this is a special sort of tribunal, not a tax court nor a criminal court. We ought to pick out those special offenses that threaten our system of justice whereby all men receive equal treatment before the law. We have already done that in the other articles.

Let me quote two of those who spoke against; they offer two different kinds of reasons for voting no. Waldie, who voted yes for each of the other four articles of impeachment, voted no on the income tax issue. His words are as follows:

I speak against this article because of my theory that the impeachment process is a process designed to redefine Presidential powers in cases where there has been enormous abuse of those powers and then to limit the powers as a concluding result of the impeachment process. And though I find the conduct of the President in these instances to have been shabby, to have been unacceptable, and to have been disgraceful even, I do not find a Presidential power that has been so grossly abused that it deserves redefinition and limiting. If there has been any abuse of a Presidential power it has been that the President may have utilized his office to cower the Internal Revenue Service from conducting a complete and thorough investigation. That has not been alleged. If that had been the case, that should have been included within article II of yesterday's action on this committee, when we were dealing with the failure of the President to faithfully execute the law.

I do find then, that this is not an abuse of power sufficient to warrant impeachment and thereby a redefinition and a limitation of that power, and I hope the article will be rejected.

Thornton, who voted yes on the first three articles, voted no on numbers IV and V. Here is his argument:

I think it is apparent that in this area there has been a breach of faith with the American people with regard to incorrect income tax returns and the improper expenditure of public funds. But it is my view that these charges may be reached in due course in the regular process of law.

This committee is not a tax court nor criminal court nor should it endeavor to become one. Our charge is serious and full enough, in determining whether high crimes and misdemeanors affecting the security of our system of government must be brought to the attention of the full House, debated there, and if found to exist, presented to the Senate. And to my view, by so doing and by bringing those serious charges to the attention of the House which we have already brought we are doing our part to ensure that this system of justice—which will enable all men to receive equal treatment before the law—will continue and can be applied in these instances which have been described to us tonight.

Waldie spoke to the theme of power; Thornton spoke about the theme of equal justice under law. Since the overall debate was brief, it is hard to judge from what was said whether Waldie or Thornton represented the majority of the committee. However, we do have the pattern of the voting, and we can make inferences from the votes. Recall that Thornton prevailed on his motion to narrow the scope of Article III. Furthermore, in the overall pattern of the votes, Thornton was more of a centrist than Waldie. Consequently, one can deduce from the voting that Thornton was more representative of the committee than Waldie. Finally, there is the evidence of Mezvinsky's speech, the major theme of which was equality in the enforcement of the law, and thus the integrity of the system. Mezvinsky's speech reads as though it was directed more toward Thornton than toward Waldie; since Mezvinsky knew his audience, we can infer that most of the committee members were more like Thornton than like Waldie.

We could, at this point, ask if those who voted no were right in their judgments; that is, was there an official act that threatened the system? I think that this question is less important than another one, namely, why define the issue that way? But it is nevertheless worthwhile to ask if they were right.

If the question is whether Nixon's tax fraud threatened our system of equal justice, one could say they were right for the simple reason that answering it either way could be called right. Given the question they asked, I can imagine myself voting either way. A deliberate underpayment of taxes could reasonably be said to be an official act, and not a personal act, for a president; it could be said that he tried to exploit the power of his office, and his cheating could endanger the tax-collecting process in a way that a private citizen's would not. On the other hand, since these judgments are matters of historical assessment and of contextual evaluation, one could reasonably doubt them. If one had doubts, then the other remedies of the law would seem more appropriate.

These differences, reasonable differences, are tolerable, but only if they are differences within the right question. The crime was serious; why should we want more? In the debates they wanted something more: not merely an act that was unlawful, but an act whose unlawfulness threatened lawfulness itself.

The most curious and interesting feature of this question is that those who asked it were using law, presupposing law, and yet they were not asking a legal question. I have used the phrase "the legal imagination" already in this book, and I have used it to characterize the distinctive quality of certain discourse in the transcript, and of the minds that produced that discourse. Here too, we are in the presence of what might be called "the legal imagination," but it is certainly not "legalistic." In order to see the distinction, one might compare the argument over Article V, which occurred on July 30, 1974, with the words spoken at the beginning of these proceedings on January 31, 1974.

Recall that a resolution was introduced. Caldwell Butler asked some questions that were legal in a particular sort of way: what effect would the resolution have in changing the scope of their authority, and would this effect in turn affect their power to issue subpoenas? John Doar avoided answering these questions by uttering legalistic obfuscations. The questions asked were lawyers' questions, and the refusal to answer them was a lawyer's mode of refusing.

Six months later the committee members had reached the end of their journey, and there had been some changes. They were no longer speaking from within the legal system, asking legal questions and acting as though the answers were decisive. They were now standing outside the system and asking whether Nixon's acts were a threat to the system of tax collecting; answering this sort of question called for some sort of "political" or "historical" judgment. Their problem was to find some way to talk about these larger problems in a coherent way. If they were to talk about more than mere illegality, if they were to talk about the sort of unlawfulness that endangers lawfulness itself, they needed a language, they needed some names for the something that was at stake.

This something, this unlawfulness that threatens lawfulness, was expressed by way of several different verbal formulas, but the two most common metaphors were that certain actions were "a threat to the system" or "endangered the rule of law." Variations on the two phrases were a common theme throughout the debates. For example, Thornton, who was one of the key members of the swing bloc of votes, defined the issue as being "to ensure that this system of justice—which will enable all men to receive equal treatment before the law—will continue." How should we interpret these words?

We know how to interpret the word "threat" when we read or hear it in phrases like "a threat of bodily harm." We have no problem with this expression because we have some reasonably clear understandings about the distinctions between healthy bodies and bodies that have been harmed. But a system, and especially a system of government, is not like a body. Breaking a rule of a system is not like breaking a leg of a body, and a system is not harmed by losing a rule the way a body is harmed by losing a leg.

As for the phrase "the rule of law," it is an especially fascinating metaphor. As a cultural symbol it is powerful, so much so that the citizens of Massachusetts wrote it into their revolutionary constitution: their aspiration was to have "a government of laws and not of men." This phrase is so routine that it is hard to look at it freshly and see how metaphorical it is. Yet one must remember that all of the acts of government are performed by humans. Since it does not seem likely that this pattern will change, it follows that governing, or ruling, will always be done by humans.

One is tempted to translate this metaphor by expanding it along these lines: we want the humans to govern via law instead of by some other means. There is no harm in saying things like this, but then they don't help much either, for it is not altogether clear exactly what the "other means" might be. One could puzzle over this point, but I think that the best thing to do is to forget the verbal formula and look at what we do.

Let us begin by turning away from constitutional law and constitutional politics and looking at religion. What sorts of things are threats to religion? Blasphemy is less threatening to religion than laughter; he who conducts a black mass concedes the power and does not ignore it, but he who giggles is making a more fundamental threat. Compare the ordinary criminal law of murder, or homicide. The ordinary murder, which as a matter of statistics is a family affair, is no threat to law, for those who kill in despair can honor the commandment that they do not obey. But imagine that there were an equally large number of people who would kill for sport, who found it amusing; the commandment would be destroyed.

These analogies are a start. They show that a norm can be broken without being endangered; and these analogies can illustrate this point because they are simple and clear. However, our system of law and government is complicated, and so we can expect difficulty in using the test that several of our representatives asserted: a crime is not an impeachable offense unless it is both a serious crime and a crime against the system of government.

In the seventeenth century, philosophers conducted their investigations into the nature of law in a civilized society by use of a particular version of the comparative method: they compared "civil society" with "the state of nature." We can follow their example in the use of metaphors by contrasting our legal system with law as it prevails on the playground. (A playground is a metaphor for "the state of nature," as that phrase is used in philosophy, and it has the advantage of being a more familiar metaphor.) The playground has its laws: don't be a crybaby; don't snitch on a kid to a teacher; and many others. For purposes of comparison, the important thing is that these rules are accepted by the citizens of the playground; whenever you or I broke such rules, we knew we had done wrong, and we tried to conceal the offense, or to make up a special excuse, or something. Moreover, the very same citizens who accept the rules also enforce them; ridicule and shunning are the normal sanctions, but fists will sometimes be used.

By way of contrast, it is not quite right to say that we accept the rules of law that are supposed to govern our conduct, and the reason is that we don't know about most of them; it doesn't seem right to say that we accept something we don't know about. I do not understand the tax code, even though I teach in a law school, and I assume that most people understand even less than I do. There is the additional complication that the rules we do know about are likely to be changed, and the tax code is a good example of this phenomenon; the little bit of tax law that I once learned has been changed. It is more accurate to say that we have officials—legislators, judges, and bureaucrats—who promulgate rules; what we accept is their authority to promulgate rules, as distinguished from accepting the rules themselves. Consequently, I read the IRS publications that explain the law, ask the advice of those who know how to translate these documents, and pay what they tell me I owe.

The contrast that I have just drawn (between a playground and the United States) may be oversimplified, but it is accurate enough to illustrate the conclusion that our legal system can be threatened more by misconduct at the secondary level of officialdom than by misconduct at the primary level of the citizenry. If you and I disobey the law, we are no threat to the system; unless our fellow citizens join with us in large numbers, there is no threat. But it doesn't take that many at the top to subvert the system.

Perhaps it is obvious enough that those at the top can subvert law in ways that we at the bottom can't, but since this phenomenon is the central issue of Watergate, and since it is also at the core of the charges against Nixon, it seems worthwhile to be more precise. First, we depend upon officials to enforce the law; indeed, this dependence is a strong one, for you and I as citizens are prohibited from enforcing the law. If we were to try, others would say that we had attempted "to take the law into our own hands." Our acts would be called "vigilante justice," and if there were enough of us, we would be called a "mob." In short, the U.S. legal system is the exact opposite of a playground. You and I had to enforce the law of the playground if it was to be the law. But in the United States the general rule is: if the law is to be the law, you and I are prohibited from enforcing it.

Secondly, when laws (norms) are not enforced, they cease to be law. This second proposition—law must be enforced to be law—is unpopular with many nowadays. Indeed, I have been assuming this principle without stating it, but I want to be explicit about it because many seem uncomfortable with this sort of claim. Perhaps it has become unpopular because it is the kind of thing that people who believe in strict retribution are fond of saying. As a logical matter, we ought not to be disturbed, for it is logically possible to believe in strict retribution and also to believe that the number of crimes should be few and the sanctions should be lenient; however, it is one of the facts of our culture that only a few among us have gone that way. We are more likely to meet up with strict retribution ideas, especially as conveyed through the mass media, traveling in the company of harsh, or even cruel, ideas about the substance of law. Consequently, when we react negatively to such ideas, we sometimes overreact; in our rejection of the cruelty of the punishment proposed, we are tempted to go further and reject the very idea of punishment.

Even so, we ought to be clear about the difference between *asking* people to do something and *telling* them that they have to do it. We are being dishonest with ourselves, and others, if we don't specify which one of these two very different enterprises we are engaged in. When others don't do what we want them to do, are we going to do nothing, admitting that they have a perfect right to refuse us, or are we going to do something about it?

This point is worth special emphasis in the context of Watergate, if we but pause to remember the aftermath of the votes taken by the thirty-eight. After the committee had voted, and after further tapes were released which were even more incriminating than those already before the committee, Nixon resigned. Consequently, the committee vote was the only vote; we never had the expected impeachment by the House nor the trial in the Senate. Furthermore, President Ford pardoned former president Nixon, and so no criminal charges were ever pursued.

My own memory of all of these events is that many people felt cheated. Nixon was not tried and convicted and punished; he was able to retire and receive all of the financial rewards that a former chief executive is entitled by law to receive. Consequently, many felt that the law was not vindicated; it was not enough that he be removed from office, for he should also suffer punishment. Interestingly enough, I even recall reading eloquent essays on the necessity for punishment by publicists who had previously, in a different context, written eloquent essays about how punishment and retribution were outmoded and barbaric impulses that are discreditable among civilized people. And I also remember that those who defended Ford regularly said that Nixon had in fact been punished and had suffered, which is an argument that concedes the necessity for punishment but claims that it had happened. I think that all of this is relevant to my thesis that there is a connection between law and punishment.

There are surely details of my arguments about law and punishment and officials that can be questioned, and if this were a formal philosophical treatise, I would attend to details. But I have not made these arguments for the sake of philosophy, but for the sake of drawing distinctions among the different articles of impeachment. The distinction that seems worth making is that between an obstruction of justice or an abuse of power and tax fraud.

Under the heading of obstruction of justice, it was alleged that Nixon condoned the paying of money to criminals so that they would keep quiet about who participated in their crime. Under the heading of abuse of power, it was alleged that he tried to use the IRS against his political enemies. There are many things that can be said about these allegations, but for the moment I am interested only in why our representatives thought that these charges were distinguishable from Nixon's tax fraud.

My own reading of the transcript is that they characterized the tax fraud as unofficial conduct that was not a threat to the system. Consequently, I understand them as saying that there is a difference between Nixon the president and Nixon the taxpayer. Furthermore, only in his capacity as president could he perform an unlawful act that would threaten the law itself. This distinction did not solve all of their problems, for even granting the distinction, there were still some difficult questions of judgment that had to be faced. However, the distinction itself is sound enough.

I hope that in this chapter I have argued persuasively that the distinction is plausible, but to recapitulate: law is not law unless it is enforced; in the United States, law can only be enforced at the official level; the president is our highest-ranking official who is responsible for enforcing the law; consequently, he can by his official conduct do more damage to law enforcement than anyone else can.

Of course, none of the above is a logical refutation of Mezvinsky's argument. He was offering a perfectly reasonable proposition when he asserted that Nixon's taxpayer actions were also, in the circumstances of the case, official actions; it is surely reasonable to say that Nixon took advantage of his official power. However, this is a question of judgment, not of logic, and so those who disagree are also being reasonable.

As for myself, although I agree with Mezvinsky on the merits, I wouldn't have voted with him. I think that he is right on the merits because I believe that the distinction between Nixon as president and Nixon as citizen is bound to come unraveled in the world of politics. When I was in law school, there was a commonly used phrase that my teachers employed when they wished to castigate distinctions such as this one: "It smells of the lamp." In other words, it is the sort of distinction that can make good sense in a scholar's study, but it won't distinguish cases in the somewhat rougher precincts of a trial court or a legislative chamber. However, granting that Mezvinsky is right about this issue, I would still dissent. In part, my dissent from him is based on my own sense of good strategy. If I were a manager for the House of Representatives at a trial in the Senate, I would prefer to focus my efforts. I would be trying to strike a balance between the advantages of focusing on the central issue and the advantages of presenting a complete picture. On balance, I would drop the tax fraud. This sense of mine about strategy, and about the relative advantages of focus versus completeness, is based upon my own experiences. I have been a prosecutor and a defense counsel, and my practice led me to believe that one must strike such a balance in presenting a case. Of course, this belief could be misplaced, for it is merely an interpretation of my own experience.

I also have a more substantial reason for parting company with Mezvinsky. As I have already conceded, I think that he has the better of the argument, given the statement of the issue. However, I am unhappy with the issue. To ask, as the committee did, whether Nixon's conduct was an official act that threatens the system of tax collection is to confine the debate too narrowly. I don't mean to criticize Mezvinsky personally; he probably would have gone into other issues most gladly, but the limits of time and his sense of his audience dictated what he could say. Were I given the power to shape the issues, I would want the debate to turn on the question of breach of trust. I would want the committee to debate other points: has the president behaved honorably, and what is the nature of his public trust? Of course, time was running out and everyone was tired; it would be unfair to judge harshly.

However, let us return to the main theme. Suppose we distinguish the tax-fraud article on the grounds that it did not involve the sort of official conduct that somehow threatens the system. What then do we do with the Cambodia article? If anything involves official conduct, it does.

ANOTHER NEGATIVE VOTE

In Article IV Nixon was charged with lying to Congress about the U.S. bombing of Cambodia. Of course, the ugly word "lie" wasn't used in the article, but the article did charge that he had concealed the facts and submitted false and misleading statements. In the debates, it was called lying: the ugly word was used. Since Congress has the sole responsibility, under the Constitution, to declare war and to appropriate money for the national defense, it was charged, and quite reasonably so, that Nixon's actions were in derogation of the lawful authority of Congress. Why, then, was this article voted down, and overwhelmingly so? Furthermore, why did the committee spend so little time on it? Recall that the debate on Article V, the tax-fraud problem, occupies forty-three pages in the printed version; debate on Article IV takes only twenty-seven.

There was no question that Nixon's conduct here was official conduct. Furthermore, the offense was serious; as Drinan put it, unlawful war making is more serious than unlawful wiretapping, and concealing a massive bombing is more serious than concealing a minor burglary.

It also seems fair to say that the offense, if proved, was an offense against the operation of the system. In the previous chapter I stated that officials can subvert law by not enforcing it. In order to make the point that I was trying to make, I had no need to distinguish among different types of officials; it was sufficient to make a hand-waving gesture toward the secondary actors whom we call officials, in contrast to the primary actors whom we call citizens. But distinctions need to be made. Different officials have different sorts of authority and responsibility; and it is a feature of our system that we have rules about the questions of authority and responsibility. It must be granted that some of these rules are matters of a generalized cultural expectations, but some of them are meant to have the sharp bite of law.

Contrast this system with the playground, our state of nature, and note how different it is. When I was a boy, there were rules about what games boys played with boys, what games girls played with girls, and what games were mixed. These rules were enforced; the rituals of shaming and shunning were used. Now the rules have changed, but there are still rules. We are all familiar with this phenomenon, and so I trust that I have described enough of it so that I can go on and point out that authority to change is not a problem. In the state of nature, there is no need to ask: who has authority to change the rules? The citizenry who accept the rules are they who enforce them; we know that the rules are rules because they are enforced; and the rules are changed by not enforcing the old rules and instead enforcing new ones.

Our polity differs in that there is a structure of cooperation among the secondary actors whom we call officials; there can be neither change nor stability in law without the cooperation of a surprisingly large number of people. In order for this cooperation to have any continuity in time, the modes of cooperation must be understood. As I see it, the Cambodia article raises these issues. By our traditions, the president has great powers of initiative in foreign affairs, but we also expect the president to get the consent of the Congress. Technically, the procedure that has been used to symbolize consent has been the appropriations process. Although we must admit that this procedure is imperfect, and so the consent given will be imperfect, still one might regard it as better than nothing. Moreover, an imperfect procedure is fragile, and if the president conceals relevant facts, submitting false and misleading statements, then it is possible that the fragile structure of cooperation will break.

These general comments can define the nature of the issue, but how can it be argued in detail? Again, I begin with a defender.

—It is clear that Nixon ordered the bombing in order to cut off a supply line of weapons and troops and thus he was acting to save American lives.

—That may give authority to act, but it can't excuse secrecy.

—But in this particular case, secrecy was a diplomatic and military necessity; the Cambodian government was willing to consent to the bombing only so long as we kept it secret.

—That may be a reason to keep it out of the newspapers, but that can't excuse lying to Congress.

—But he didn't do that; selected key members of Congress were told what was going on.

—Now wait a minute; you claim that thirteen members of Congress were told, but three of them are dead, three have denied being told, most have only a vague recollection of anything, and only four definitely recall being told about the bombing.

—Well, that sounds good for the president; the evidence is indefinite, and the burden of proof is on the proponent of impeachment.

—Of course, but on what issue? What you are confused about is that the president doesn't get to say how he notifies Congress; he has to follow the procedures that Congress has specified.

—If you mean the War Powers Resolution, remember that it comes after these events.

—No, I don't mean that. I mean the regular procedure that we use for the CIA, for nuclear weapons, and so forth: the "classified line item" procedure.

—Aren't you getting hyper-technical? You know that if he had asked, the Congress would have approved.

—I don't know, because he didn't ask. And by the way, about the War Powers Resolution, the Congress didn't declare any new powers for itself by that; the Constitution itself gives us the final say.

—If so, why have so many presidents done things like this? The whole course of our history has been the expansion of presidential power.

—Are you saying that what is, is right? We have had usurpation of power, and it's time we did something about it.

Granted that the argument goes something like that, how can we step back from it and evaluate it? First, there are no real disputes about the facts. Everyone agrees that false statements were submitted and that they were submitted on the president's orders. There are disagreements about the larger historical context, about how to fit these acts together with other acts, but even these differences seem smaller the more often I reread the debate.

Conyers led off the debate for the proponents:

> We have said here again and again during the course of these deliberations that the one power of the Congress that might, in fact, be even more powerful than that which brings us here is the power to declare war. And I think that we might make an observation about the nature and importance of this proposed article from the outset, because as one who has worked with all of the members who have labored toward an understanding and a support of any of the articles, I want to extend first my commendations to the chairman and then to those who composed the "fragile coalition" because I have been as concerned as any about putting it together and keeping it together.
>
> So far during these proceedings, no one has been required to make any compromises of conscience that have to do with those measures that should be considered as impeachable offenses, and I think that to do anything less would demean these proceedings and leave us open for criticism for all time in the view of those who will study in great detail our conduct during this historic event. And, so I bring this article forward not with some trepidation, because it seems to me first of all to have been that matter which underlies all of the articles that have been voted on so far, because we have stated time and time again that the reason for Watergate and its coverup, and the incursions into the various agencies and departments of Government was motivated by a necessity that was political.
>
> Well, I would like to suggest to you that the reason that that political motivation arose in the first place was the fact of the Vietnam war, in which this Cambodian incursion is an incident, because this President, unfortunately, like the one before him, is to a greater extent a casualty of the Vietnam war. And I would point out to you that we need to state only the matter quite simply. Tapes are not required. It is not necessary that we go beyond the documentation that has been put together by the committee and analyzed. The President unilaterally undertook major military actions against another sovereign nation and then consistently denied that he had done so to both the Congress and the American people.
>
> Now, my colleagues, I suggest that the consequences of that conduct are so enormous for us assembled here not to seriously consider this as an additional article, not to merely add articles upon articles but as one of the most important that go to the perhaps most important duty that befalls us in the Congress.
>
> You know, many people don't know or have forgotten who has the author-

ity to declare war in 1974 in the United States. Many people have forgotten that the Congress constitutionally has that sole authority. And so I would urge that we in an attempt to reassert those powers which we consider to be vital and precious, if the constitutional form of government is to prevail and continue and improve, that we give the gravest consideration to this article.

Now, I know that there is something else that is troubling us and I am constrained to speak frankly to it because there are members who, regardless of how much agreement that they may give to the arguments that will be presented by myself and the proponents, feel that perhaps they have some implication in the result of undeclared wars and I think a word should be said about it.

I don't think that we can absolve the fact that the Congress has failed to declare officially that war that has haunted us for nearly 10 years but that we can use this moment as a new beginning, as a point of departure where the Congress says from this moment on, from this day forward, we will reinstitute that law constitutionally asserted from the beginning that somehow during the course of previous administrations, I am frank to admit, has eroded and we find that that power is no longer ours and ours alone.

To me, the most interesting part of Conyers's argument is his historical analysis. He argues that the Watergate burglary, the cover-up that was the obstruction of justice, and the general pattern of abuse of power all had their source in the events of Article IV. On Tuesday, July 30, the sixth and last day of the debates, he asserts this connection rather briefly. In his opening statement, on the second day, which was Thursday, July 25, he was more expansive. In that opening statement he was not arguing for a vote; he was explaining to his colleagues the context of the matter before them, which was Article I. His words were:

It is my view the reason we must now consider to vote and to impeach Richard Nixon goes far beyond the scope of the resolution of impeachment before you and what I would like to do here is describe from my view the backdrop against which the complaint against the President now requires us to vote out this limited narrowly drawn bill of impeachment.

Richard Nixon, like the President before him, is in a real sense a casualty of the Vietnam war, a war which I am ashamed to say was never declared. Since these hearings began on May 9 we have had a professional staff of some 89 men and women gather in great detail over 42 volumes of information that was considered throughout some 57 sessions. The study of the 42 volumes of carefully compiled documents and papers and testimony revealed clearly the pressures of an administration so trapped by its own war policies and the desire to stay in office it was forced to enter into an almost unending series of plans for spying and burglary and wiretapping inside this country and against its own citizens without precedent in American history.

The President took the power of his office and under the guise of protecting and executing the laws that he swore to uphold, he abused them and in so doing he has jeopardized the strength and integrity of the Constitution and laws of the land and the protections that they ought to afford all of the people. This is why we must exercise this awesome power of impeachment, not to punish Richard Nixon, because the constitutional remedy is not punitive, but to restore to our Government the proper balance of constitutional power and serve notice on all future Presidents that such abuse of conduct will not now or ever again be tolerated.

I would like to turn back to 1969 when the war was still going on and the President was confronted with the option of attempting to bomb through infiltration routes the pass in the Far East through at least two independent sovereign nations, Laos and Cambodia, and when that decision was made to bomb Cambodia, on May 9, 1969, or shortly thereafter, William Beecher, the Pentagon correspondent for the New York Times, published a story that ran a headline that said "American B-52 bombers in recent weeks have raided several Vietcong and North Vietnamese supply dumps in Cambodia for the first time," and that story triggered off the beginning wiretaps because shortly thereafter the administration embarked upon a series of illegal surveillance and involving both members of the press and of the Government that were unparalleled.

It was more than just a wiretapping between friends and government but it was the beginning of a policy of corruption that started then and spread to three different levels because it embraced, first of all, a decision not to entrust to the American people the true and difficult nature of the war policy that this administration had embarked upon. And second, it was so caught up with that policy that it was ready to deceive the elected representatives of the Congress on what we were doing and what we were supposedly voting money for. And third, and logically, the outcome of the first two, is that the administration finally could not even trust themselves. And so we are confronted with the record of friends tapping friends and of paranoia that shows even no trace of conscience.

And so this secret war in Cambodia which seemed at first incidental, as I studied the record before us, has to me begun to be the string around which we can understand the tremendous amount of surveillance and spying and burglary that has characterized the evidence, and I consider that to be evidence now, that is before us.

Witness the deception that the President practiced on the Congress and the American people when from May 17, 1969, he approved a secret bombing campaign personally that as a result caused more than 150,000 air strikes to take place and more than 500,000 tons of bombs dropped upon a neutral nation. And yet, 2 months after that date in which he had personally authorized this conduct, the President said: "I have tried to present the facts about Vietnam with complete honesty and I shall continue to do so."

In a news conference 6 months later he stated that the people of the United States were entitled to know everything they could with regard to any involvement of the United States abroad. A year after the bombing began he declared, "We respect Cambodia's neutrality and we hope that whatever government prevails, they will recognize that the United States' interest is in the protection of its neutrality."

And so, my friends, it seems to me that that marked the beginning of the intelligence-gathering activity which under his direction or on his authority is unparalleled. These activities involved widespread and repeated abuses of power and illegal and improper activities by the executive agencies and, of course, wholesale violations of the constitutional rights of citizens.

Drinan also supported Article IV:

Let's see first what this document or article does not do. This document takes no position whatsoever on the merits of the war in Indochina. We are not asking hawks and doves to vote along that line today. This resolution makes provision for those who feel as others do who have spoken here. If they feel that the bombing in Cambodia saved American lives, they can continue with that conviction and still vote for this resolution today.

This resolution relates in its essence to secrecy, secrecy in the executive branch of government. General Wheeler testified on July 30, 1973, that the President personally ordered him not to disclose the bombing in Cambodia and I quote General Wheeler: "To any member of Congress."

This article is very narrow. This article means that we don't want a President authorizing or ratifying the concealment in the Congress of the facts about a certain situation concerning which the Congress must act. The Founding Fathers I think we should not [sic] made a provision in Article I that the Congress itself must publish a journal except in a narrow exception the journal could be secret if the Congress so decided. There is no provision for secrecy in the executive branch of government whatsoever in the Constitution. The whole history of secrecy in government was the very thing that the Framers of our Constitution wanted to undo.

Secrecy means that we in the Congress don't get the essential information that we need in order to legislate. In the area of war, Madison said that the war-declaring power in Congress must include everything necessary to make that power effective. . . .

Those who want the Congress to stand up in the future will say, I am never going to allow another President to ratify the concealment from the Congress of basic facts and give to the Congress false and misleading statements about anything domestic, about anything foreign, especially about bombing operations in a neutral nation. . . .

The central argument of the defenders was that because Congress over a considerable period of time had accepted and condoned presidential encroachments on its powers, that inaction made it questionable whether invoking the impeachment remedy in this instance was appropriate. Cohen's argument against Article IV is typical of those who defended the president on this theory:

The basis, as I understand, for this article is that this constituted a usurpation of power by the President, power properly belonging to the Congress. And I do not think that anyone here will contest that. I think the bombing was wrong, because it was done secretly, and it was done without Congress' consent.

But, while this usurpation may have taken place, I happen to believe that the usurpation has come about not through the bold power of the President, but rather on the sloth and default on the part of the Congress, because over the years, there was a good 10 years that Congress failed to take very strong action in this area in which we have the ultimate and sole control. So, what happened after the bombing was disclosed and what action did Congress take at that time? I can recall my first year in Congress standing in the hall listening to the countdown on the vote where that Congress finally determined to cut off the bombing in Cambodia. And I could not help but be impressed with the electricity in the air. For the first time, Congress was finally going to regain the powers that it had given up, again through its own sloth and default.

So, what happened is that last year Congress, rather than condemning the President for past actions, they actually went ahead and ratified it in my opinion. They passed legislation which would have allowed the President to continue to bomb for an additional 45 days.

Now, that to me was tantamount to ratifying a past act, and I cannot see us imposing a double standard upon the President of the United States after having some complicity in this act. We come awfully close to the margin when we pass a law which says it is all right to bomb just for another 45 days but after that you cannot bomb, and besides, we are going to impeach you for what you have done before.

Now, that is what happened. I know the gentlelady from New York [Holtzman] did not share in that vote, nor did I, and a number of others on this committee did not, but the fact of the matter is that Congress did have some complicity. . . .

The logic of this position must rest, if at all, on a notion that rules should be promulgated, that no one should be charged with an offense unless the norms by which the case is to be judged have been declared. In cases like these, when one wants to know which rules have been declared or promulgated, it is certainly fair to say that one can look to practice, to custom. One can argue, and it is a fair argument, that a president is entitled to rely upon the precedents of what presidents customarily do, particularly when the Congress has customarily consented to those precedents. If one argues in this way, it is fair enough to conclude that by the then existing rules, what Nixon did was marginally wrong, but only marginally so.

Sometimes it is necessary to improvise rules as we go along, and in such cases we may need to apply them to someone who lacks notice. But it is one thing to improvise when we are faced with the unanticipated and another when what has happened is something that everyone knows about and that has been happening all along. Furthermore, the Congress would not here be improvising from a position of neutrality, as mediators, arbitrators, and sometimes judges do, since the Congress was a participant.

In short, the logic of the rule of law permits but does not compel the conclusion that the norm that Nixon was charged with violating was not in fact a norm of our system. So if one judges Nixon by the logic of the metaphor, then one should decide against this article. However, if the norms of democracy seem more compelling, then support of this article is perfectly logical.

Comparing Articles IV and V, it looks as though one is dismissed for being too legal and the other for not being legal enough. Article V was too legal: it charged a criminal violation of the tax code, but that is all that it did; many of those who voted no appear to have thought that there were no larger historical and political implications. Article IV was not legal enough: what was done had plenty of political and historical implications; these implications were frightening; but Nixon did what many presidents have done and so did nothing that was against the rules.

On a good day I can see the logic of all of this, but most of the time it doesn't satisfy me. What is good about it is that there seems to be implicit in this pattern of voting a recognition that law and politics are not two separate realms, divided by an impermeable boundary. A recognition of this interconnectedness is a recognition of reality, and therefore is good. In addition, I can understand the pattern of these two no votes as an interpretation of our culture by a group of politicians with a professional stake in being right about such things. As I read it, they might have been interpreting our culture in this way: any judgment that they made had to rest on both law and politics, and it might not rest on either one of them singly. If they judged Nixon solely on the law, then our cultural definition of that step would likely be that they had been legalistic and thus avoided talking about what was really important. If they judged Nixon solely in political terms, then they risked the cultural definition that they had been partisan and had merely acted so as to take revenge against him. In this context I can understand the advantages of the rule of law as a metaphor, for it seems to offer a way to avoid these risks. Indeed, by requiring that there be unlawfulness, and further that this unlawfulness be a threat to lawmaking, they seem to have found a technique for uniting law and politics.

As I have said, on a good day I can assent to all of this reasoning. Unfortunately, for any of it to be real in the world, it has to be enacted and as I examine the actual performance, I am less than pleased. In discussing Article V, I said that the distinction "smelled of the lamp" in that context. As for Article IV, I am not persuaded by the argument that Nixon did nothing unlawful. Indeed, I tend to get impatient and start snorting when that sort of argument is made. I think that the

constitutional rule is clear enough, and I have this conviction because I am convinced that Drinan's account of the eighteenth-cen-
tury understanding of the document is accurate.

Drinan's account is contained in his opening statement, which he
made on the second day of the debates, Thursday, July 25:

> Mr. Chairman, members of the committee, in the long summer of 1787 at
> the Constitutional Convention in Philadelphia, the delegates from my own
> State of Massachusetts consistently opposed the inclusion of impeachment
> in the Constitution. Massachusetts argued on July 20 of that year that
> American law, unlike that of England, would provide for a genuine separa-
> tion of powers, judicial review, and regular elections by the people. Hence it
> was argued, the remedy of impeachment which had been frequently abused
> in England would not be necessary in America.
>
> The delegates of Massachusetts furthermore reasoned on that day that
> impeachment would [not?] impose a penalty which would make known to
> all citizens the punishment that they could expect for their offenses. Mas-
> sachusetts in that year wanted America to aspire to the ideals already stated
> in the constitution of Massachusetts, "a Government of laws and not of
> men."
>
> Only South Carolina voted with Massachusetts to omit impeachment
> from the Constitution. Massachusetts then, as so often since, stood almost
> alone.
>
> During this summer, Mr. Chairman, I have wondered countless times
> whether or not the delegates from Massachusetts in 1787 were after all cor-
> rect in their judgment that impeachment was unnecessary, unwise, and in-
> deed dangerous.
>
> My concern over this question has deepened as I have witnessed the pro-
> cess of selecting articles of impeachment on the basis of whether they will
> fly.
>
> I have been troubled because the process of choosing articles of impeach-
> ment is not necessarily done in the order of their gravity but to some extent
> on their capacity to "play in Peoria."
>
> There has been no shortage of lawless acts on which to focus in this
> inquiry. But only history will discover why the greatest deception and pos-
> sibly the most impeachable offense of Richard Nixon may not become a
> charge against him. I speak of the concealment of the clandestine war in
> Cambodia. I do not here speak of the claimed merits of the bombing. I speak
> only of its concealment. We see in this series of events the same abuse of

power and the same techniques of coverup employed by the President and his associates in the aftermath of Watergate. . . .

Congress and Congress alone had the right and duty to judge whether the United States was justified in making or not making war on Cambodia. President Nixon, in my judgment, usurped that right from the Congress.

Can we be silent about this flagrant violation of the Constitution? Can we impeach a President for unlawful wiretapping but not impeach a President for unlawful warmaking? Can we impeach a President for concealing a burglary but not for concealing a massive bombing? . . .

In and around my congressional district in eastern Massachusetts there live the descendants of those who fought at Concord and Lexington. Those American revolutionaries two centuries ago took up arms in a desperate and determined effort to gain the precious right of knowing and participating in the processes of their own Government.

The men who fought in the revolution at Concord and in the other 12 colonies gathered in Philadelphia from May 25 to September 17, 1787. They came together to create a Government where no one ever again would have to enter into an armed rebellion to indicate his right to be free of tyranny, and for the Framers of the Constitution the ultimate tyranny was war carried on illegally by the Executive without the knowledge or consent of the Congress.

Mr. Randolph of Virginia stated in the Constitutional Convention that the President under the Constitution that they were writing would have great opportunities of abusing his power, particularly in the time of war.

Against that ultimate tyranny, the authors of the Constitution adopted impeachment as the ultimate remedy.

Within 1,000 days we as Americans will commemorate the 200th anniversary of that fight for freedom that began on the rude bridge at Concord. We will be worthy of those who fought on our behalf in 1776 if we fight for the rule of law as they set it forth in what is now the oldest written constitution still in use in the entire world.

Finally, Mr. Chairman, we will be worthy of those who brought freedom to America only if we continue to remember as we have in this inquiry that impeachment is designed as the one way by which a President can vindicate himself. Col. George Mason reminded the Framers of the Constitution that the impeachment proceeding is designed to vindicate the rights of the people against a tyrant but it is also provided so that there will be honorable acquittal for a public official should he be unjustly accused. Whatever the outcome of this proceeding, the American Government will be purified and strengthened and in that process all of us will become as never before free men in a free society.

It is true that the executive department had not adhered to the original understanding of its limits, but it had overstepped those limits for reasons of expediency. It is also true that legislators had not tried to enforce the rule concerning war powers, but they had refrained for lack of political courage. In this context, it seems to me that a Congress with courage and integrity was entitled to enforce the original understanding. However, I do believe that a no vote could have been an honorable act. Accepting everything that Conyers and Drinan said, a member of Congress might have responded: "Yes, Nixon is guilty, but so am I, and it would be the rankest sort of hypocrisy for me to vote to impeach." I can respect that response. All of this makes for a difficult moral problem for Conyers and Drinan. As I understand their political careers, they were free from personal guilt in this matter; unlike most of their colleagues, they had not encouraged the president to usurp power in this realm. However, they may perhaps have shared some institutional guilt: having fought and lost, they may in some way have been bound. There are no easy answers to this sort of quandary, and I would sympathize with them whichever way they resolved it.

As I assess the arguments, I judge the no vote on Article IV to be analogous to the vote to narrow the scope of Article III. McClory's theory for Article III and the Conyers-Drinan theory for Article IV both proposed that Nixon should be impeached because he usurped the power of Congress; in each instance it was claimed that the usurpation was impeachable because it weakened democracy; both times a majority rejected the argument. Article III passed, but only after its scope had been narrowed; it appears that it passed because of the link between the defying of the subpoenas, as charged in Article III, and the obstruction of justice and abuse of power, as charged in Articles I and II. Throughout, the metaphor of the rule of law was preferred to that of democracy.

7 THE ABUSE OF POWER

Earlier in this book, starting with the opening passages of the transcript, I advanced the claim that the talk was lawyer's talk. But the lawyer's talk that became crucial by the end was talk about the rule of law; Nixon was charged with doing something that threatened the lawmaking process.

As we consider the charges of abuse of power and obstruction of justice, the talk about the threat to law is more complicated. In the context of Article V, the issue was relatively simple; it was argued that Nixon's refusal to pay his taxes could endanger the tax-collecting process. In my gloss of this argument, I asserted that law depended on enforcement and that those at the top could destroy law by not enforcing it. These assertions go to the existence of the legal system, but they do not capture all of what we mean by the phrase "the rule of law."

There is a difference between having a legal system and having a rule of law. Any moderately complicated political unit will have a legal system, and the reason is obvious enough: it is more efficient that way. Indeed, it is hard to imagine how a government can govern without promulgating some general rules. However, it is very easy to imagine (since we have historical examples) a government that governs by rules that bind citizens only, not officials. Do public officials make rules that bind others, or are they also bound? Especially crucial in this regard are the rules that define the authority to make rules. Do public officials accept these limiting rules, or are these limits up for grabs? An answer to this question determines the nature of politics, and the issues are more complicated for the abuse-of-power charges of Article II than for the tax-fraud charges of Article V. For tax fraud, the rules at stake are rules about the duty to pay taxes; for the abuse of power, the rules are about the power to make rules. These secondary rules, rules about making rules, are important in many ways; law and politics intersect on their terrain.

If the limits on power are accepted, politics can go forward within the limits of the rules that define power. Given this sort of politics, a successful politician gains certain kinds of power, and we all know what he or she has won. Coalitions must be set up, since no one person has enough power. Once a coalition has been formed, we can know what sort of power it has won; for example, we can say whether a coalition has won the power to tax or not to tax, or the power to kill or not to kill.

Alternatively, politics can be about the rules that define power. In its classic form, this sort of politics is called revolution. Politics can be directed toward eliminating the office of king or commissar and substituting a new office with different powers.

These alternatives are perhaps too starkly drawn. Politics can include taking the powers of an office and making something new of them; this case may fall somewhere in between. Granting this possibility, we must consider how we can understand it. For example, in our time, many say that the office of the presidency has become "imperial." Has it? And if so, how has it happened? More particularly, can we judge when a president has overstepped his power, or abused his power?

Rightly or wrongly, this judgment was made about Richard Nixon; the affirmative vote on Article II was a vote to impeach him for abuse of power. This article charged that Nixon had attempted to misuse the IRS and the FBI by having them conduct investigations for political purposes; it charged, too, that he set up a secret investigative unit (colloquially known as the Plumbers, since its job was to stop the "leaks" of secrets) that was financed by campaign contributions and used for improper purposes.

The debate on Article II does not have the dialectical interplay that I have set out in my presentation of the last three articles. In those articles there was some argument over what happened, but the real argument in each case was whether it was an impeachable offense. Consequently, the thrust and parry of the interchange could be presented in a dramatic form. With Article II there was a real debate over what happened; and furthermore, the debate had to be about this factual question, for the defenders conceded that if Nixon had done what he was charged with doing, then it was impeachable.

For example, take the wiretaps and the bugging that are charged in subparagraph (2). The charge was the he had misused the FBI and the Secret Service by directing them "to conduct . . . electronic surveillance"; the most important part of this charge is the statement that it was done "for purposes *unrelated* to national security, the enforcement of laws, or any other lawful function of his office" (emphasis added). The defenders' first move was "to put it in context." The nation was at war in Vietnam at the time, and there were negotiations under way to bring that war to an end. We also were negotiating with the Soviet Union to establish some limits on "strategic" (or nuclear) weapons. As always, there were leaks, which the defenders of Nixon characterized as "massive," which they said endangered national security, and which they claimed the president had a duty to stop. The defenders conceded that perhaps there were some irregularities and excesses, but one doesn't impeach for such things.

Those who proposed impeachment accepted one of the premises of this argument: The president may authorize warrantless wiretapping for national security purposes. However, they did not believe that these were his motivations; they argued that Nixon ordered the wiretaps for reasons of personal and partisan politics. As evidence, they pointed to certain facts: wiretaps were put on journalists who had no information about national security matters; wiretaps were put on people who had long since left the government; statutory procedures were not followed; and in particular, the files for these wiretaps were removed from the FBI and put in the White House. From evidence of this sort, they concluded that the "electronic surveillance" was done "for purposes unrelated to national security."

If we accept the fact that wiretaps were set up for political purposes and not for national security purposes, we must ask what follows, what sort of issue it is. The contrast with the tax-fraud problem is rather striking. In that case it was charged that a secondary official (Richard Nixon the president) was refusing to honor a primary rule (that Richard Nixon the taxpayer had to pay his taxes). In the wiretap events a secondary official (Richard Nixon the president) was refusing to honor secondary rules (the procedures for conducting wiretaps).

In order to read the debate, one must thread one's way through some procedural complications. There were several drafts of Article II. The "official" version was offered, as per custom, in Donohue's name; but Hungate offered a substitute which had been negotiated by several of the most influential members of the committee, and the debate was on the Hungate substitute.

The procedural maneuvers for the debate break down into five stages. First, Wiggins offered a "point of order"; he noted that Article II did not charge any violations of criminal statutes, and he argued that it followed from this fact (and it was a fact) that the article did not state an impeachable offense. After an impassioned reply by Danielson, Rodino overruled the point of order, saying that this was the ultimate issue on the merits, on which the House and Senate would have to rule.

The second stage was opening remarks. Hungate, Hutchinson, and McClory offered their views on the merits. However, this general debate was abandoned. Under the rules of parliamentary procedure, as propounded in Jefferson's manual, motions to amend have precedence over the main motion, and so the chairman recognized Wiggins, who opened the third stage of the debates by offering several amendments. The Wiggins amendments would have altered certain details of the wording, and the spirit behind these amendments was to tighten up the proof requirements concerning Nixon's personal role. The debate swirled around several issues, such as Nixon's knowledge before the fact, his ratification after the fact, his duty to supervise, and so forth. The issues were not sharply posed, since there was some confusion over whether the amendments merely spelled out in more detail what was already said or whether they were meant to make a change. The amendments were defeated, but one cannot be sure about the rationale behind the vote.

In the fourth stage of the debates, there were a series of "motions to strike." This technique, the motion to strike, was used to focus debate on specific charges. Article II has numbered subparagraphs specifying particular abuses of power, that is, subparagraphs charg-

ing illegal wiretaps, attempted misuse of the IRS, and the establishing of a secret investigative agency as a part of the White House staff.
Motions were made to strike each of these subparagraphs, and so
there was a debate on the merits of each of these charges. Each of the
motions to strike was defeated.

The fifth and final stage of the debate was the general debate. Having disposed of specific charges, the members debated the article as a
whole. The final act was the vote, and in accordance with parliamentary technicalities, it was actually two votes: there was a vote to
replace the official draft with the Hungate substitute, and then there
was a vote to approve the final version.

I would now turn to the merits, using the jargon of "secondary"
and "primary" that was introduced in Chapter 6. Recall that primary rules are the rules of peaceable behavior that you and I as primary actors, as the citizenry, are to observe in our daily intercourse.
The secondary actors, the public officials, are supposed to make and
enforce these rules; and the rules that say how they should go about
the job of making and enforcing are the secondary rules. The distinctive feature of the wiretap problem is that the legislative, executive, and judicial branches of our government all share power in the
making of the rules for wiretapping. Nixon's actions can be understood as a challenge to the accepted allocation of power, as a defiance
of the norms for sharing the authority to make the rules. The tax-
fraud problem is, in contrast, a simple enforcement issue.

The debate about the misuse of the IRS is analogous in that it too
starts off being about a question of fact. Not all of the facts are disputed: there is no disagreement that presidential aides attempted to
get confidential information from tax returns to be used for political
purposes; the aides attempted to have audits and investigations
started against the political opponents of the administration. There
is also agreement that the top officials of the IRS resisted, so that,
generally speaking, the plan was frustrated.

The disputed question is Nixon's role in all of this activity. Did he
know what his aides were doing? If he knew before the fact, why
didn't he stop them? If afterward, why didn't he reprove them and
discipline them? Dean has testified that Nixon knew, and so there is
argument about the president's credibility. There are some tapes of

conversations in the Oval Office, and so there is argument about how to interpret the language on these tapes.

I am not interested in the details, but what is striking is that the question is about Nixon's state of mind. This is a striking parallel to the FBI charge. Again the committee members are arguing about why Nixon did what he did: did he intend it for good purposes? Again they are arguing about his knowledge: did he know that his subordinates were acting for bad purposes?

The extreme version of this argument is made by Sandman. In sum, Sandman says that he does not think himself naive, but he believes that every man who has been elected president has to have been a good man, or else the people wouldn't have elected him. Since the president must be a good man, then Sandman wants to believe that the president must have done what he did for a good purpose; and for impeachment there must be overwhelming proof that what was done was not done in the best interests of the country. Here are his words:

Now, at the outset I don't think I am the most naive person in the world, but I like to believe that every man that has ever been President of the United States had to be a good man and he had to be a great man or this great country would have never voted for him to be the leader of this country. It may be a surprise to some in this room but the President I was extremely fond of that I had the good fortune to know as everybody in the room did was not a Republican. It was Lyndon Johnson. And I thought it was a horrible thing during the Bobby Baker talks that some people thought, well, maybe we ought to try to impeach LBJ. That was wrong, and I hoped it would never start.

Now, anybody who feels this way, and I kind of think the country feels this way, they would like to believe their President is a pretty good man, and to do otherwise or prove to them otherwise, it would take a tremendous amount of proof to do that, and it should, tremendous. You can't do this loosely. And this is important. The whole world is watching this proceeding and what we do, we had better do right, because the effect of it is going to make a precedent for 1,000 years.

That is the importance of the question as I see it. And because of this, it disturbs me when I try to think of some of the problems involved, the Ellsberg break-in and whatnot. I think maybe we are a little bit mixed up and maybe we ought to sit down for a moment and review where we are.

I was on a program one time in Long Island. I walked in the room with a very famous man, a good Democrat, Senator Muskie. He got a pretty good hand. I am sure no one in the audience knew me. But what applause there was, I say they did it because of him. And then behind Senator Muskie, by about 3 or 4 minutes, walked in Daniel Ellsberg, one of the panelists on our program, and believe it or not, the stadium shook and I wondered why. Why did that happen? Here is a man who confiscated secret documents [the so-called Pentagon Papers, a review of the war in Vietnam] and against the law of the Nation he dispersed these documents. I thought that was wrong. And I couldn't understand why this fellow came in there like a hero. But he is. This is a strange thing happening in this country.

And now as a result of that [the Plumbers had broken into the office of Ellsberg's psychiatrist], a mistrial was declared in that case [the criminal prosecution against Ellsberg for releasing the Pentagon Papers] and a man who is as surely guilty as guilty can be was never declared guilty, was never penalized, and instead we now talk about impeaching the President of the United States.

I think our thinking is a little fuzzy here and maybe we ought to sit down and look over that once again and make sure we are doing the right thing. Is it more popular to give away secret documents than it is to protect the security of a great nation? I don't think so. And I would like to believe in the absence of extremely heavy proof that what the Chief Executive did he did for a good purpose, and this is why I have the strong feelings in the direction that I have and that is why I have argued the way I have in this proceeding.

I don't take my obligation here any more lightly than any other person and I believe that what we are doing here, we are acting as a judiciary in a sense. We are judging whether or not the President of the United States should be replaced. We are judging the rights that he has as an individual as well as a President and it is not in line with what at least I learned in the 20 years that I went to school that he has any less rights than any other American, and no one can ever make me believe that due process still isn't the law of this land and it is always going to be the law of this land. And for these reasons I think we have to not make an inference against the President of the United States, if anything we have to make an innocent's—an inference that what he did he did in the best interests of the country. This is what I would rather believe.

While the committee members are arguing this question, they do not say why the state-of-mind issue—that is, whether Nixon acted from good motives or not—is so important. However, throughout the debate broader questions of principle are brought forward, and they connect the issue of Nixon's motives with other topics. From what I have already covered, you can imagine several possibilities: they could talk about balance of power, criminality, breach of trust, or the threat to the rule of law. By now, it should come as no surprise that the proponents of impeachment talk a great deal about the rule of law.

For example, they point out that the wiretaps endanger the security of the home, which is guaranteed by law; if wiretapping is done as a reprisal for speaking against Nixon's policies, then it endangers the freedom of speech that is guaranteed by law; and the misuse of the IRS threatens the right to equal treatment under the law that is the fundamental key to the whole system of ideas about law.

All of this seems familiar enough, as rhetoric about the rule of law and about the connection between law and liberty, but what does any of it have to do with the question of fact—Nixon's state of mind—about which the committee argued so intensively? If he invaded our rights, then he invaded our rights. We wonder whether we need to care why he did it. One possible reason why we should care is that our rights are defeasible; we have rights, but they must yield at times when the national interest demands it. Consequently, if Nixon were acting in good faith, if he were honestly in pursuit of national security, then we would not regard the wiretapping as a bad thing. Certainly, there is much in the debate that supports this understanding of the connection.

However, another argument is advanced by Flowers, one of the "swing men" of the middle block of votes. The core of his argument is as follows:

You know, my friends, a fundamental principle of our Government is that equal justice under law is a guarantee of every citizen. To put it another way, we are a Government of laws and not of men.

This commitment to equal justice was written down in a few places, like in our Constitution, and in our laws, and in some court decisions. But, I think just as important are some commitments to this principle that must be assumed in our society.

For instance, the assumption that the sensitive agencies of Government with peculiar power over each one of our citizens, like the police power, and the power to tax, will not be abused or misused for political purposes. This is a fundamental source of the people's confidence in our Government.

That the President and his men should have trifled with this source seems to me to be sufficiently grave to qualify as a component of an article of impeachment.

When he uses the phrase "peculiar power," one is puzzled, since the power to tax and the power to enforce laws by using the police are not "peculiar" to the process of government, but are the rock-bottom basis of government. What is peculiar about the IRS and the FBI? Or more to the point, what is peculiar about them in the context of the rule of law?

What is peculiar is how much of what is most important about these agencies is ungoverned by law. Of course, if an agent of the FBI says that someone has committed a crime, we can have due process of law in determining whether that person is guilty or not guilty. However, there are things that happen before the processes of law are invoked, and they are important. First, there is the decision to investigate. It could be based on a hunch, on rumor, or on malevolence. Inevitably, there is something arbitrary about it, for there are always more crimes to be investigated than there are investigators, and at the beginning there is seldom any compelling reason to go one way instead of the other. This arbitrariness of the starting place does not always apply to local police, who may start with crimes of violence. But for the more subtle crimes that the FBI generally investigates, and even more so for the tax evasions that the IRS must try to uncover, the decision to start is rarely obvious.

Moreover, once the investigation has begun, its pace and scope can vary. Agents can be hasty or dilatory. Their search for evidence can be a narrow probe or wide-sweeping. And thus the potential for difference in investigations is enormous. Furthermore, as the hunch at the beginning is replaced by evidence, it is not usually obvious which inferences should be drawn. Agents will differ in how they evaluate, what crimes they drop or add, and thus what turns the investigation should take.

None of these things would be a problem if there were no harm in being investigated, if the only harm that might be caused came from being convicted of a crime or of tax evasion. But we know that that is not the case. There is a cost in being investigated, without regard to the outcome, although it is hard to generalize about these possible harms. One may have to spend money and time on defense. The psychological strain can be debilitating. Reputation can be destroyed. However, none of these harms are legal harms; that is, one can't sue or get any compensation for them.

We are left with a problem: the process of investigating can cause great harm; the decision to investigate is subjective, as is its scope; there are no legal remedies for an unjustified investigation. Consequently, if the power to investigate is abused, then the executive can easily defeat the value of certainty, that repose in the security of liberty which Flowers believes to be part of the set of values symbolized by the phrase "the rule of law." Here we have a value that must be preserved by the executive department. The judiciary cannot handle it, and if it has been threatened by the executive, only the legislature can give a remedy.

All of this can be put more abstractly, more philosophically, as an answer to two questions: What does the rule of law mean to our legal culture? And how should we understand the connection between good and bad motives and the rule of law? In the simplest situation, that in which the same group of people make and enforce their law, and do so without using formal structures, the whole notion has no play. Only when we get specialization, even if it is just temporary, do we begin to get circumstances in which the use of this phrase can make any sense. If we have an assembly that has enacted what we might call a statute, and if there are executive officers who have a duty to enforce the statute, we can begin to speak of the rule of law, and we might mean to be drawing a distinction about different kinds of executive action: is the executive official executing the policy of the assembly, or his own policy? Of course, it might be a difficult empirical question to say which has occurred, but that is another matter, one which we can sidestep.

Whatever might be the merits of this version of the rule of law (the executive does what the assembly wants done), it was not what was primarily at stake in Watergate, and so we need not inquire into the conceptual and empirical issues that are raised by it. In order for the charge against Nixon to fit into this version of the rule of law, one would have to say that there were statutes passed by the Congress that he was refusing to enforce, or that he was enforcing statutes in a way that was inconsistent with the obvious meaning of the language of the statute, or something similar.

Charges like these are part of the debate on Article II, but only a minor part. Although this sort of charge is serious, it is not what is serious about Article II. The serious charge, according to Flowers, is that there has been selective enforcement of the law for political purposes. The selective enforcement of a statute is an altogether different sort of thing from the enforcement of a statute in a way that is inconsistent with its meaning. For example, if the IRS agents had done the tax audits that Nixon's aides asked them to do, they would have observed the meaning of the taxing statutes in both substance and procedure. Even so, there would have been selective enforcement, since the targets of these audits would have been chosen for political reasons. Consequently, we can see how Nixon's state of mind—his motivation—is relevant; it is a crucial fact in judging whether there has been selective enforcement and thus a failure in the rule of law.

What is serious about Watergate is the danger to law that selective enforcement can cause, especially when selections are made to get revenge on political enemies. In complicated legal systems such as ours, citizens do not know very much of the details of the law that bear upon their lives, and a fortiori, what they don't know about they can't consent to. Assuming that legitimacy rests upon consent, it is obvious that consent to law in our culture does not mean consent to the rules of law that impinge upon our lives. Since consent to law cannot very often rest upon consent to the actual content of our law, it follows that in complicated legal systems such as ours, the citizen's consent cannot be very substantial or real, and thus it is likely to be fragile. In this context selective enforcement can threaten respect for and consent to the law. As Flowers says, the offenses specified in Article II threaten "a fundamental source of the people's confidence in our Government." Although most of us might agree to this thesis, it is worthwhile to try to be clear about why it holds true.

Since citizen consent is not consent to the rules that bear upon life (as I have already argued, we generally do not know the law), any consent must be directed toward something else, about which there seem to be two possibilities: without regard to the rules, the citizen might accept the political results that the executive and the judiciary are reaching; or without regard to rules or results, the citizen might accept the authority of judges and officials to do what they do. In short, a citizen might accept either authority or its visible results, without knowing or caring anything about the rules that are part of the system.

We must then ask: what danger can there be that cheating on the rules (a selective enforcement and disingenuous interpretation) will lessen the authority of the law? If there is cheating, it is evidence that the officials do not deserve the trust the citizens may have in them, and if it becomes widely known, citizens will not accept their authority, unless certain crude methods that are rather common in our century are used. But since our citizens, by hypothesis, do not know much about the rules of the system, the only sort of cheating that they are likely to learn about is selective enforcement, which is likely to be visible at the level of results. Selective enforcement is thus more dangerous than disingenuous interpretation, since it is more likely to be visible.

These things do seem to have been involved in Watergate, but one should note that the potential for harm from selective enforcement was greater than the actually achieved harm. The attempt to misuse the IRS was frustrated; had it been successful, harm would have been done, not just threatened. The illegal wiretaps by the FBI did cause harm, but so long as it was still secret, it did not cause the average citizen to lose trust. Similar things could be said about the Plumbers.

However, with these distinctions about potential harm and actual harm acknowledged, we can return to the topic of how we might talk about these harms. There is no problem in stating the ultimate conclusion. We can say that this misuse of the power to investigate is not a faithful execution of the law, and that this is wrong because the Constitution imposes upon the president the duty to execute the laws faithfully. Furthermore, faithful execution of the law is part of what we mean by the rule of law; all of this follows from what has already been said.

Granting the reasoning so far, there is still room for further argument. The failure to execute the law faithfully can be seen as related to other things, such as liberty or democracy. For example, when the Plumbers broke into the office of the doctor who was Daniel Ellsberg's psychiatrist, and when it was established that they were seeking derogatory information about him that might be used to discredit him in the public eye, and when the motivation for this act was found to be their dislike of him because of his role in making public the Pentagon Papers, and when we understand the break-in as an attempt to destroy him as a person for what he did, in place of any attempt to hold him liable in a court of law for what he did, how then shall we condemn this act of the Plumbers?

One way to condemn it is to emphasize the private rights that have been invaded. Ellsberg had a right to confidentiality, and that right was threatened. The psychologist had a right to be safe from trespass into his office, and that right was clearly violated. Furthermore, had the Plumbers been successful in finding what they were seeking, and also in remaining undetected, they might have been able to invade two other rights held by Ellsberg: his right to his reputation and his right to receive a fair trial.

Another way to condemn the break-in is to emphasize the harm that was done to the political process. Statutes had been passed by the Congress that were arguably relevant to what Ellsberg did. (On this point I want to be prudent, or at least cagey, and say that there are some "interesting" questions of statutory interpretation, and that depending on how they are resolved, he could have been criminally liable.) However, what the Plumbers did led the trial judge to declare a mistrial in the Ellsberg case. Consequently, the members of the Congress and the public do not know what they are entitled to know about the legal problems with these statutes. Furthermore, the public was entitled to make judgments about the political wisdom of the statute and of Ellsberg's acts. Ellsberg was entitled to appeal to the public and organize around the issue, and the same rights of appeal to the public were held by Nixon. The Plumbers succeeded in derailing and frustrating any public political process that might have resembled that to which we are entitled.

For each of the items that have been listed under the heading of abuse of power, a similar sort of analysis could be made. We could talk about the invasion of private rights of liberty, or we could talk about damage to our power to participate in politics. The failure to honor the rule of law can be important in both of these two ways, in relation to our private liberties and to our public politics.

How did the thirty-eight talk? Both sorts of things were said, but as I read the transcript, the emphasis was on the private rights of liberty: the rule of law was seen as valuable because it is a way to secure our liberties; there was not much talk about the rule of law as a way of empowering us to participate in a democracy. Let me quote Edwards, who gave an especially clear statement of the thesis that an abuse of power is bad because it threatens our liberties:

Mr. Chairman, I would like to speak just for a few minutes about all of article II, which I suggest is an expression of our deep devotion to the Constitution, and above all, to the first 10 amendments, known as the Bill of Rights.

Article II is our rededication to and our reaffirmation of the Bill of Rights and the principle that no officer of our Government from the most lowly to the highest can violate with impunity those fundamental constitutional rights guaranteed every American citizen.

In 1787 when the 13 Colonies were considering ratification of the new Constitution, three of the new States voted to ratify only on condition that a recommendation for a Bill of Rights be added. These men remembered well that they or their parents had fled from the kingdoms of Europe to seek individual freedom in the New World. They had just finished winning a war to insure this independence and freedom, and they were not about to substitute a new Federal Government for the old tyranny without safeguards designed to protect their rights as individual human beings from the arbitrary encroachments of the new Government. So it was that the First Congress of 1789 enacted the Bill of Rights as the first 10 amendments to the Constitution.

Jefferson in a letter to Madison urged the adoption and said, "Let me add that a Bill of Rights is what the people are entitled to against any government on earth."

Why do I review this history this late at night in the consideration of article II? It is, of course, because article II charges President Nixon with intentional violations of the Constitution, chiefly amendments one, four, five, and six.

The first amendment guarantees freedom of speech and of the press. In direct contravention of this amendment, President Nixon authorized or permitted illegal wiretapping and other surveillance of individuals, including reporters, and the use of this information so gained for political reprisals and defamation.

The fourth amendment guarantees the rights of people to be secure in their homes, their houses, their papers, against unreasonable searches and seizures. In direct contravention of this amendment, President Nixon established a special investigative unit within the White House to engage in searches and seizures without legal warrant, and the special White House unit committed a burglary in the State of California.

The fifth amendment guarantees to all equal protection of the laws. In direct contravention of this amendment, President Nixon endeavored to use the Internal Revenue Service for tax investigations and tax harassment of political opponents.

The fifth and sixth amendments guarantee a fair trial in all criminal prosecutions. In direct contravention of these amendments, President Nixon and his subordinates leaked information unfavorable to a criminal defendant, withheld information necessary for his defense, and during the trial even offered the judge a high Government position.

No proposition could be more profoundly subversive of the Constitution than the notion that any public official, the President or a policeman, possesses a kind of inherent power to set the Constitution aside whenever he thinks the public interest, or to use the more popular term now given such easy currency, the "national security" warrants it.

That notion is the essential postulate of tyranny. It is indeed the very definition of dictatorship, for dictatorship is simply a system under which one man is empowered to do whatever he deems needful for the whole community.

We look now beyond the walls of this committee room to every citizen, rich or poor, white or black, brown or yellow, from the most powerful to the humblest, and say to all who will listen, this article II is the only meaningful way to protect your constitutional rights, your right to speak what is in your mind without fear of reprisal or other harassment and your right to hear and read what others would say to you; your right to be secure in your home and your office against Government wiretappings and burglaries; and your right to equal treatment under law without fear or favor from the Government; your right, if legal difficulties should enmesh you, to a fair trial; your right to be left alone to pursue life, liberty and happiness free from unlawful incursions at all levels of government from the President down.

Of course, there were other voices. McClory, who urged a broad version of Article III, the subpoena article, took a similar view of Article II:

I would like to be recognized at this point to discuss generally this proposed article of impeachment. It seems to me that this really gets at the crux of our responsibilities here. It directs our attention directly to the President's constitutional oath and his constitutional obligation. There is nothing mysterious about this, and there is nothing evil and malicious about it. It directs the attention directly to this responsibility that is and has been reposed in the President.

This certainly is no bill of attainder. We are not thinking this up as an offense and then charging the President with a violation of it. We are calling the President's attention to the facts that he took an oath of office, and that he had in his oath of office a solemn obligation to see to the faithful execution of the laws.

This is quite different and distinct from the elements of criminality that are involved in article I charging the President with a conspiracy, and with all kinds of criminal acts of misconduct and obstruction of justice and so on—an article which I did not support because I do not believe the facts support that kind of charge.

Now, some of those who have been expressing themselves in support of article I, clearly have included feelings of deep hostility, and bitterness and political bias. On my part, article II, based on the take care clause of the Constitution which specifies a solemn obligation of the President to take care to see to the faithful execution of the laws, I want to make perfectly clear that I harbor no malice, I attribute no evil thoughts or conduct to the President of the United States. I express no bitterness, no hostility. What I do want to make clear is that the President is bound by his solemn oath of office to preserve, protect, and defend the Constitution, and to take care to see that the laws are faithfully executed.

While many of the paragraphs contained in article II may appear similar to those that are found in article I, which I opposed, it is important to note carefully that the pattern of conduct which is delineated in article I is quite distinguishable from that in article II. For one thing, I would point out there is no clear proof of conspiracy in the fact that others surrounding the President have been guilty of acts of gross misconduct. However, there is a clear violation of the President's responsibility when he permits multiple acts of wrongdoing by large numbers of those who surround him in possession of greatest responsibility and influence in the White House.

The establishment of the Plumbers, and many of the activities attributed to them are wholly unrelated to the Watergate, and that is the same case with respect to his misuse of the FBI and the CIA and the IRS. Nothing to do with Watergate for the most part. But, these are clear acts of misconduct which, it seems to me, are important for us to take note of. In other words, the acts and conduct upon which I feel an article of impeachment should be presented to our colleagues is strictly constitutional, which relates narrowly and directly to the President himself and his personal oath of office.

While this article may seem less dramatic and less sensational than the Watergate break-in and coverup, it is nevertheless a positive and specific responsibility, and a positive and responsible approach to our power on our part as investigators of misconduct.

One purpose of the impeachment process, it seems to me, is to set a constitutional standard for persons occupying the office of the President. Thus, if we approach our task in constitutional terms, we will be setting such a standard. I view the duty of the House of Representatives as something other than serving as a district courthouse to hold the President accountable for statutory violations of the criminal law. I think we can agree that the President should not commit crimes, but if we are to set a constitutional standard, we must take a different view of the facts. We must phrase our charges in constitutional terms so that the Presidents to come may know what is meant by our action. If we are to establish our proceedings as a guide for future Presidents, we should speak in terms of the Constitution and specifically in terms of the President's oath and his obligation under the Constitution. It will be of limited value to admonish a future President not to obstruct justice or engage in a coverup. However, it will aid future Presidents to know this Congress and this House Judiciary Committee will hold them to an oath of office and an obligation to take care to see that the laws are faithfully executed.

I realize that there is no nice way to impeach a President of the United States. I realize also that the distinction between the criminal conspiracy theory of article I and the purely constitutional aspects of article II may be misunderstood. But, as a member of this committee, the most I can do is to exercise my independent judgment and to search deeply my own conscience. Both reason and wisdom dictate the judgment I am going to make in support of this article II is right.

However, most of the members seemed to align themselves with Flowers and Edwards, not McClory.

Surely, no one should be surprised that the emphasis was on liberties instead of powers, and one might even surmise that our representatives were representative in tilting this way. Are our fellow citizens more interested in pursuing their private lives or in fulfilling their public responsibilities? Would they feel that they had lost more if they lost some of their privacy than if they lost some of their political power? I don't know the answers to these questions, but our representatives have spoken as though we value liberty more than power.

Perhaps this was the realistic way to talk. In an era like ours, marked by the presence of the mass media and the giant corporation, any talk about the ancient rites of democracy can seem quaint. Perhaps we should limit ourselves to worrying about our private liberties because that is all we have left to worry about. Even so, when it is put that bluntly, one pauses.

However, my words may be too strong, too harsh; I may be oversimplifying. In addition to talk about the rule of law and political participation, there is the third alternative, the *tertium quid*, of breach of trust. Recall that Sandman said that the crucial issue was Richard Nixon's good character and that he was willing to trust in it. A majority disagreed with him, but they seem to have agreed that he stated a crucial issue, since the topic of Nixon's character was a recurrent theme throughout the debates. One can interpret the allusions to Nixon's character as evidence that members of the Judiciary Committee were serious about the breach-of-trust issue.

Of course, character is also relevant to the rule-of-law question. The argument goes as follows: in order to prove a selective and politically biased enforcement of law, one needs to prove motivation, that is, to find out why Nixon did what he did; and Nixon's character is relevant to the issue of motivation. However, one need not read the debates on Nixon's character as limited to this rather narrow question. In equity, the concepts of a trust and the fiduciary responsibility of a trustee are broad enough to include more than narrow questions about motivation. Let me try to show how broader issues are relevant in equity.

The thirty-eight members of the Judiciary Committee were all lawyers, and so it is likely that most of them had read the famous words of Benjamin Cardozo, written when he was chief justice of the New York Court of Appeals. The great Cardozo, in ruling upon the sort of fiduciary duty that a partner owes to a co-partner, wrote: "Many forms of conduct permissible in the workaday world for those acting at arm's length, are forbidden to those bound by fiduciary ties. A trustee is held to something stricter than the morals of the market place. Not honesty alone, but the punctilio of an honor the most sensitive, is then the standard of behavior." Unfortunately, Cardozo's high standards have not been enforced in equity, although it is also fair to say that many have felt guilt and shame for these lapses. At any rate, if one accepts Cardozo's opinion, character is a mode of executing an office, and it demands more than eschewing bad faith and evil motives.

Of course, I do not mean to suggest that the members of the Judiciary Committee judged Nixon by Cardozo's standard. However, it is an aspiration for the office of the presidency to which they might assent, and the best evidence that they might hold such an aspiration is the tone of sadness present in their debate. All told, I think that the themes of character and trust are present in the debate, but as a muted undertone and not as the main topic. My own prejudice is that they should have been the main topic.

8   WATERGATE,
NARROWLY SO-CALLED

We come at last to Watergate proper. Five men broke into the office that was used by the Democratic National Committee as its headquarters. Using legal jargon, we can call this act a "burglary," as that word is defined by the criminal code for the District of Columbia. We also have some other legal words that are relevant, words such as "accessories" and "co-conspirators." We can use these additional words to extend the net of criminal liability to include all those aided in its commission. We can use the words "accessories" and "co-conspirators" to hold criminally liable those who recruited the burglars, those who financed the operation, those who planned and directed the entry. And finally, there are those who obstructed the investigation, those who were "accessories after the fact." It was charged that Nixon obstructed justice, and it is possible to talk about this event using a purely legal vocabulary.

However, a criminal offense need not be approached in any narrowly legal way, and especially not when the context is impeachment. The so-called cover-up (to use a nontechnical term) can be described in lawyers' jargon as conspiracy to obstruct justice, and it can be treated as a crime, but we need not say that Nixon should have been impeached *because* his participation was criminal. We can say that something more is at stake.

We need not set up polar dichotomies and declare that there are two mutually exclusive ways of talking about the cover-up. It is true that what happened was criminal, and the fact of its criminality is and was important. But we can also say that there was more involved than criminality, and furthermore, we can believe that the something more is what was really important.

If you read Rodino's opening remarks, you can see him struggling

to say what this something more might be. The date is July 24; it is
7:45 P.M.. The procedure has been set: Donohue is to introduce a
draft of Article I (plans are already in place to replace it with another
version after the staff has polished it up some more), and then each
member of the committee is to be allowed fifteen minutes to talk
about impeachment. Before getting the proceedings under way,
Rodino and the senior Republican, Hutchinson, are to make prefa-
tory remarks. Given the context, everyone talks about impeachment
in general; the committee members do not limit themselves to Article I; rather, they talk to the more fundamental question of what is
at stake.

First I wish to quote Rodino's speech; then I shall analyze it in
more detail.

Before I begin, I hope you will allow me a personal reference. Throughout
all of the painstaking proceedings of this committee, I as the chairman have
been guided by a simple principle, the principle that the law must deal fairly
with every man. For me, this is the oldest principle of democracy. It is this
simple, but great principle which enables man to live justly and in decency
in a free society.

It is now almost 15 centuries since the Emperor Justinian, from whose
name the word "justice" is derived, established this principle for the free
citizens of Rome. Seven centuries have now passed since the English barons
proclaimed the same principle by compelling King John, at the point of the
sword, to accept a great doctrine of Magna Carta, the doctrine that the king,
like each of his subjects, was under God and the law.

Almost two centuries ago the Founding Fathers of the United States reaffirmed and refined this principle so that here all men are under the law,
and it is only the people who are sovereign. So speaks our Constitution, and
it is under our Constitution, the supreme law of our land, that we proceed
through the sole power of impeachment.

We have reached the moment when we are ready to debate resolutions
whether or not the Committee on the Judiciary should recommend that the
House of Representatives adopt articles calling for the impeachment of
Richard M. Nixon.

Make no mistake about it. This is a turning point, whatever we decide.
Our judgment is not concerned with an individual but with a system of
constitutional government.

It has been the history and the good fortune of the United States, ever since the Founding Fathers, that each generation of citizens, and their officials have been, within tolerable limits, faithful custodians of the Constitution and of the rule of law.

For almost 200 years every generation of Americans has taken care to preserve our system, and the integrity of our institutions, against the particular pressures and emergencies to which every time is subject.

This committee must now decide a question of the highest constitutional importance. For more than 2 years, there have been serious allegations, by people of good faith and sound intelligence, that the President, Richard M. Nixon, has committed grave and systematic violations of the Constitution.

Last October, in the belief that such violations had in fact occurred, a number of impeachment resolutions were introduced by Members of the House and referred to our committee by the Speaker. On February 6, the House of Representatives, by a vote of 410 to 4, authorized and directed the Committee on the Judiciary to investigate whether sufficient grounds exist to impeach Richard M. Nixon, President of the United States.

The Constitution specifies that the grounds for impeachment shall be, not partisan consideration, but evidence of "treason, bribery, or other high crimes and misdemeanors."

Since the Constitution vests the sole power of impeachment in the House of Representatives, it falls to the Judiciary Committee to understand even more precisely what "high crimes and misdemeanors" might mean in the terms of the Constitution and the facts before us in our time.

The Founding Fathers clearly did not mean that a President might be impeached for mistakes, even serious mistakes, which he might commit in the faithful execution of his office. By "high crimes and misdemeanors" they meant offenses more definitely incompatible with our Constitution.

The Founding Fathers, with their recent experience of monarchy and their determination that government be accountable and lawful, wrote into the Constitution a special oath that the President, and only the President, must take at his inauguration. In that oath, the President swears that he will take care that the laws be faithfully executed.

The Judiciary Committee has for 7 months investigated whether or not the President has seriously abused his power, in violation of that oath and the public trust embodied in it.

We have investigated fully and completely what within our Constitution and traditions would be grounds for impeachment. For the past 10 weeks, we have listened to the presentation of evidence in documentary form, to tape recordings of 19 Presidential conversations, and to the testimony of nine witnesses called before the entire committee.

We have provided a fair opportunity for the President's counsel to present the President's views to the committee. We have taken care to preserve the integrity of the process in which we are engaged.

We have deliberated. We have been patient. We have been fair. Now, the American people, the House of Representatives, the Constitution, and the whole history of our Republic demand that we make up our minds.

As the English statesman, Edmund Burke said during an impeachment trial in 1788: "It is by this tribunal that statesmen who abuse their power are accused by statesmen and tried by statesmen, not upon the niceties of a narrow jurisprudence, but upon the enlarged and solid principles of state morality."

Under the Constitution and under our authorization from the House, this inquiry is neither a court of law nor a partisan proceeding. It is an inquiry which must result in a decision—a judgment based on the facts.

In his statement of April 30, 1973, President Nixon told the American people that he had been deceived by subordinates into believing that none of the members of his administration or his personal campaign committee were implicated in the Watergate break-in, and that none had participated in efforts to cover up that illegal activity.

A critical question this committee must decide is whether the president was deceived by his closest political associates or whether they were in fact carrying out his policies and decisions. This question must be decided one way or the other.

It must be decided whether the President was deceived by his subordinates into believing that his personal agents and key political associates had not been engaged in a systematic coverup of the illegal political intelligence operation, of the identities of those responsible, and of the existence and scope of other related activities; or whether, in fact, Richard M. Nixon, in violation of the sacred obligation of his constitutional oath, has used the power of his high office for over 2 years to cover up and conceal responsibility for the Watergate burglary and other activities of a similar nature.

In short, the committee has to decide whether in his statement of April 30 and other public statements the President was telling the truth to the American people, or whether that statement and other statements were part of a pattern of conduct designed not to take care that the laws were faithfully executed, but to impede their faithful execution for his political interest and on his behalf.

There are other critical questions that must be decided. We must decide whether the President abused his power in the execution of his office.

The great wisdom of our founders entrusted this process to the collective wisdom of many men. Each of those chosen to toil for the people at the great forge of democracy—the House of Representatives—has a responsibility to exercise independent judgment. I pray that we will each act with the wisdom that compels us in the end to be but decent men who seek only the truth.

Let us be clear about this. No official, no concerned citizen, no Representative, no member of this committee, welcomes an impeachment proceeding. No one welcomes the day when there has been such a crisis of concern that he must decide whether "high crimes and misdemeanors," serious abuses of official power or violations of public trust, have in fact occurred.

Let us also be clear. Our own public trust, our own commitment to the Constitution, is being put to the test. Such tests, historically, have come to the awareness of most peoples too late—when their rights and freedoms under the law were already so far in jeopardy and eroded that it was no longer in the people's power to restore constitutional government by democratic means.

Let us go forward. Let us go forward into debate in good will, with honor and decency, and with respect for the views of one another. Whatever we now decide, we must have the integrity and the decency, the will, and the courage to decide rightly.

Let us leave the Constitution as unimpaired for our children as our predecessors left it to us.

Rodino's speech has three parts; that is, the rhetorical structure of it can be broken into three parts. It has an introduction, a middle, and a conclusion: he states some general matters, then covers the particular question before the committee, and then moves back to the general again. He starts by saying that he has been guided as the chairman by a simple principle, the principle that "the law must deal fairly with every man," and he goes on to claim that this principle is "the oldest principle of democracy" and that it "enables man to live justly and in decency in a free society." Although Rodino does not say it, we can read this preface as a critique of Nixon and thus as a suggestion that Nixon has not been guided in the execution of his office by such a principle. Perhaps it is an overreading to do so: it does seem unlikely that Rodino consciously chose his opening words as an artful and subtle critique of Nixon, but it is plausible that some unconscious association could have generated what he said. More important, we can understand these words as being critical even if they were not intended to be critical.

If Rodino's principle is a critique of Nixon, then let us consider what kind of principle it is. As we might expect, Rodino does not offer definitions and analysis. Instead, he does something far wiser: he restates it and gives examples, so that we can get some contextual understanding. For example, he traces it historically, saying that it was "established" by Justinian and "proclaimed" in the Magna Carta. He restates the English version as "the doctrine that the king, like each of his subjects, was under God and the law." As for our own Constitution, Rodino asserts that "the Founding Fathers of the United States reaffirmed and refined this principle so that here all men are under the law, and it is only the people who are sovereign." As these excerpts show, he states the principle in several ways, but the variations are minor.

Rodino's use of history seems to be a way of elevating the issue: we are not dealing with a doctrine that is merely a legal doctrine; we have one of the fundamental principles of Western civilization. It would even be wrong to say that it is a doctrine of constitution law, since Rodino makes it sound even more fundamental; rather, it sounds like the sort of doctrine that lies beneath constitutional law, that can be used to create constitutional law.

With these words as an introduction, Rodino now begins to make the transition to the matter before the committee. Consistently with the high ground of principle that he has already taken, he states that the committee is concerned not with Nixon as an individual but "with a system of constitutional government." In light of all of this, it should come as no surprise that Rodino glosses the constitutional phrase "high crimes and misdemeanors" as referring to "offenses . . . incompatible with our Constitution." Furthermore, he is able to build a bridge between the constitutional language that defines impeachment and the constitutional language that prescribes the oath for the president: the Founders had experience with monarchy, and they were determined to have a government that would be "accountable and lawful"; to this end, they drafted an oath that the president must take; and so the committee has investigated for seven months "whether or not the President has seriously abused his power, in violation of that oath and the public trust embodied in it."

Rodino captures the spirit of the matter by quoting from Edmund Burke: " 'It is by this tribunal that statesmen who abuse their power are accused by statesmen and tried by statesmen, not upon the niceties of a narrow jurisprudence, but upon the enlarged and solid principles of state morality.' "

Rodino next turns away from the high ground to a new topic. At first it is not apparent that he is making a turn, for he announces that "this inquiry is neither a court of law nor a partisan proceeding." Given what has gone before, we nod, expecting the alternative to be "a constitutional inquiry" or "a high state tribunal." Consequently, it is with some shock that one reads: "It is an inquiry which must result in a decision—a judgment based on the facts." As a turn in the argument, the move from principles to facts is puzzling; Rodino does not say what the principle is that makes these facts more important than other facts, and so we will have to figure it out for ourselves.

At this point, let me repeat the crucial language verbatim:

In his statement of April 30, 1973, President Nixon told the American people that he had been deceived by subordinates into believing that none of the members of his administration or his personal campaign committee were implicated in the Watergate break-in, and that none had participated in efforts to cover up that illegal activity.

A critical question this committee must decide is whether the President was deceived by his closest political associates or whether they were in fact carrying out his policies and decisions. This question must be decided one way or the other.

It must be decided whether the President was deceived by his subordinates into believing that his personal agents and key political associates had not been engaged in a systematic coverup of the illegal political intelligence operation, of the identities of those responsible, and of the existence and scope of other related activities; or whether, in fact, Richard M. Nixon, in violation of the sacred obligation of his constitutional oath, has used the power of his high office for over 2 years to cover up and conceal responsibility for the Watergate burglary and other activities of a similar nature.

In short, the committee has to decide whether in his statement of April

30 and other public statements the President was telling the truth to the American people, or whether that statement and other statements were part of a pattern of conduct designed not to take care that the laws were faithfully executed, but to impede their faithful execution for his political interest and on his behalf.

The second paragraph of this excerpt states a precise factual question that one might call one of "the niceties of a narrow jurisprudence." Indeed, this paragraph is a restatement of the criminal law question: was the president a party to the conspiracy to obstruct justice? If this were all there were to impeachment, then the Judiciary Committee would be doing the same thing a court of law could do.

However, in context, it is fair to say that Rodino is posing a larger question. The first paragraph refers to a public statement, and the third paragraph returns to this public statement; the question as thus posed is whether the president was deceived or was deceiving. But this is not the whole problem; there is more to it than saying that the president was part of a conspiracy and furthermore that he lied about it. Instead, Rodino goes on to say that these things raise another factual question about "a pattern of conduct." Regarding this pattern, Rodino poses two possibilities: either Nixon was taking care that the laws were faithfully executed or he was impeding their execution "for his political interest and on his behalf." In other words, Rodino is saying that the committee must determine whether (1) Nixon conspired, (2) he lied about doing so, (3) he did these things for his own political interest, and (4) this was a regular pattern of conduct in the execution of his office.

Rodino is right about one thing: the question that he has posed is a question of fact. But it is not a narrow question of fact; we could call it a broad question of fact, in that it is a question about a "pattern of conduct," as distinguished from a particular act. One can say that the three elements of conspiring, lying, and seeking a personal political interest are not important either by themselves or as combined; the key is that they were part of a pattern of conduct, and this pattern is what amounts to a breach of the oath of office. But we must ask why this is the case, and what principle makes it an impeachable offense.

Perhaps we should interpret Rodino's speech by noting that these four paragraphs have a logical and rhetorical structure that makes some of the facts seem more important than others. The first of the four paragraphs starts with a public statement that Nixon had made to the American people, and the fourth paragraph states that the crucial issue is whether this statement was a telling of the truth. This rhetorical structure allows us to interpret Rodino's statement so as to understand that lying about the cover-up was more blame-worthy than having participated in it. We can assimilate this judgment to the equitable metaphor of a trust, since in equity we expect the trustee to make an accounting: a trustee must disclose truthfully what has been done.

In making this interpretation, we can emphasize the ending of the fourth paragraph. In this paragraph Rodino is attempting to summarize, to restate, and so he begins: "In short, the committee has to decide . . ." Having posed first a finding that would be in favor of Nixon, he then states a finding that would be grounds for impeachment, namely, any conclusion that Nixon did what he did "for his [own] political interest and on his [own] behalf." In those words we have the very core of the notion of a trust. A trustee is someone who acts on behalf of another, the beneficiary; for the trustee to engage in self-dealing on his or her own behalf is a clear breach of trust. Of course, I may be guilty of giving these four paragraphs more prominence than they should have. I am partial to the breach-of-trust metaphor, and my prejudice in its favor may be misleading me. At any rate, one speech alone does not constitute a consensus; one must consider more.

Each member of the Judiciary Committee made an opening statement, and like Rodino, each one ranged into broad issues and did not limit the scope of the statement to the questions raised by Article I. Consequently, these statements took some time. Of the six days spent in final debate, two days were spent on these opening statements; they constitute 24 percent of the volume that contains the final debates. The debate on Article I itself takes up about 33 percent of this volume.

In their own way, these speeches were among the most dramatic events of the Watergate affair, but they did not have anything flashy about them. What was so dramatic was the seriousness of it all, the understated intensity of what was said. It was different from the normal sort of seriousness with which politicians pronounce upon the world. Normally, their way of being serious involves so much playacting that it is likely to strike one as merely pompous. But not this time. I was reminded of Dr. Johnson's famous quip that the prospect of being hanged in a fortnight tends to concentrate the mind. For the average member of Congress, having to vote on impeachment was the same sort of thing.

Railsback spoke for many of his colleagues when he said: "Let me say, Mr. Chairman, that I used to like to be on the House Judiciary Committee when we were worried about penal reform and juvenile delinquency, trying to improve some very important things in our country that needed improving. But, I am about to reconsider my assignment now that we have had amnesty, abortion, impeachment and now a bomb threat." They had to vote, but they would have been happy if the need could have somehow just gone away.

The drama of the speeches was in part a function of timing, for the Supreme Court issued its opinion in the case of *United States* v. *Nixon* on July 25, the first of the two days set aside for the committee's opening statements. Nixon had said that he would obey only if the Supreme Court's decision were "definitive." It was unanimous; he was ordered to turn over the tapes. Was "unanimous" the same thing as "definitive"? There were hours of silence, and then it was announced that Nixon would comply. These accompanying events tended to increase the committee's tension and thus to increase the dramatic effect of the speeches.

If I were to analyze the opening speeches as I have the rest of the final debates, this book would get long and tedious. But is is unnecessary to do so, for I have already given the ideas that were presented in the opening statements. These statements prefigured the whole debate; I have chosen to present them as they were acted upon in later votes, since proceeding in this way makes it possible to clarify the meaning of the statements in the context of the votes. For example, Drinan made the argument that the bombing of Cambodia was the most important and serious charge that could be brought; Conyers offered his historical analysis of the dynamics that led up to Watergate; and their opening statements thus prefigured what they would say as proponents of Article IV. Similarly, Mezvinsky, who led the proponents of Article V, argued in his opening statement that Nixon's tax evasion was an impeachable offense. McClory led the proponents of Article III, which charged that Nixon's refusal to honor the committee's subpoenas was an impeachable offense, and so there is no surprise in discovering that he took a strong position about this point in his opening statement, even though he did not explicitly say that he would vote for impeachment.

Many memorable words were said during the two days of the opening statements. It seems a shame to pass them by, though to discuss each one in detail would take too long, and to pick out a few might seem unfair. However, one speech in particular seemed to capture the imagination of all its hearers. I refer, of course, to Barbara Jordan's. Like many such speeches, it doesn't read all that well, and we can find in this fact a confirmation of something that serious students of rhetoric have often asserted: the spoken word is a dramatically different form of expression from the written word. It lacks in the reading the sonorities of her wonderful voice, the strength of her face, the physicality of her vibrant presence.

Even so, one can read with "the third ear" and recapture some of the effect. Picture if you can a strong, black woman speaking in a voice that is recognizably Texan and yet unlike the routine accents of that state; imagine her starting off in this way:

Earlier today we heard the beginning of the Preamble to the Constitution of the United States, We, the people. It is a very eloquent beginning. But when that document was completed on the 17th of September in 1787 I was not included in that "We, the people." I felt somehow for many years that George Washington and Alexander Hamilton just left me out by mistake. But through the process of amendment, interpretation and court decision, I have finally been included in "We, the people."

This sort of beginning is risky, for there is a real danger of sounding mawkish. But she took the risk, for she wished to make the claim that the long, historical struggle to be included among the citizenry gave the Constitution some special meaning to her. She did not want to lose it now. And so her speech was filled with history. One of the ways in which she used history was to quote from the great names of the past and then juxtapose the conduct of Richard Nixon with the noble ideals of the statesmen who wrote on the criteria for impeachment. My own judgment is that this technique was what made her speech so impressive and what justified the risk of the way she began. It came down to the contrast between the nobility of her language (both her own and that which she quoted) and the actuality of Nixon's conduct.

The balance of Jordan's speech is as follows; I recommend that instead of reading in silence, you try to hear it:

Today, I am an inquisitor, I believe hyperbole would not be fictional and would not overstate the solemnness that I feel right now. My faith in the Constitution is whole, it is complete, it is total. I am not going to sit here and be an idle spectator to the diminution, the subversion, the destruction of the Constitution.

"Who can so properly be the inquisitors for the nation as the representatives of the nation themselves?" (Federalist No. 65) The subject of its jurisdiction are those offenses which proceed from the misconduct of public men. That is what we are talking about. In other words, the jurisdiction comes from the abuse of violation of some public trust. It is wrong, I suggest, it is a misreading of the Constitution for any member here to assert that for a member to vote for an Article of Impeachment means that that member must be convinced that the President should be removed from office. The Constitution doesn't say that. The powers relating to impeachment are an essential check in the hands of this body, the legislature, against and upon the encroachment of the Executive. In establishing the division between the two branches of the legislature, the House and the Senate, assigning to the one the right to accuse and to the other the right to judge, the Framers of this Constitution were very astute. They did not make the accusers and the judges the same person.

We know that nature of impeachment. We have been talking about it awhile now. "It is chiefly designed for the President and his high ministers" to somehow be called into account. It is designed to "bridle" the Executive if he engages in excesses. "It is designed as a method of national inquest into the conduct of public men." (Hamilton, Federalist No. 65) The Framers confined in the Congress the power if need be, to remove the President in order to strike a delicate balance between a President swollen with power and grown tyrannical; and preservation of the independence of the Executive. The nature of impeachment is a narrowly channeled exception to the separation of powers maxim, the Federal Convention of 1787 said that. It limited impeachment to high crimes and misdemeanors and discounted and opposed the term, "maladministration." "It is to be used only for great misdemeanors," so it was said in the North Carolina ratification convention. And in the Virginia ratification convention: "We do not trust our liberty to a particular branch. We need one branch to check the others."

The North Carolina Ratification Convention: "No one need be afraid that officers who commit oppression will pass with immunity."

"Prosecutions of impeachments will seldom fail to agitate the passions of the whole community," said Hamilton in the Federalist Papers No. 65. "And to divide it into parties more or less friendly or inimical to the accused." I do not mean political parties in that sense.

The drawing of political lines goes to the motivation behind impeachment; but impeachment must proceed within the confines of the constitutional term, "high crime and misdemeanors."

Of the impeachment process, it was Woodrow Wilson who said that "nothing short of the grossest offenses against the plain law of the land will suffice to give them speed and effectiveness. Indignation so great as to overgrow party interest may secure a conviction; but nothing else can."

Commonsense would be revolted if we engaged upon this process for petty reasons. Congress has a lot to do. Appropriations, tax reform, health insurance, campaign finance reform, housing, environmental protection, energy sufficiency, mass transportation. Pettiness cannot be allowed to stand in the face of such overwhelming problems. So today we are not being petty. We are trying to be big because the task we have before us is a big one.

This morning in a discussion of the evidence we were told that the evidence which purports to support the allegations of misuse of the CIA by the President is thin. We are told that that evidence is insufficient. What that recital of the evidence this morning did not include is what the President did know on June 23, 1972. The President did know that it was Republican money, that it was money from the Committee for the Re-Election of the President, which was found in the possession of one of the burglars arrested on June 17.

What the President did know on June 23 was the prior activities of E. Howard Hunt, which included his participation in the break-in of Daniel Ellsberg's psychiatrist, which included Howard Hunt's participation in the Dita Beard ITT affair, which included Howard Hunt's fabrication of cables designed to discredit the Kennedy administration.

We were further cautioned today that perhaps these proceedings ought to be delayed because certainly there would be new evidence forthcoming from the President of the United States. There has not even been an obfuscated indication that this committee would receive any additional materials from

the President. The committee subpena is outstanding and if the President
wants to supply that material, the committee sits here.

The fact is that on yesterday, the American people waited with great anx-
iety for 8 hours, not knowing whether their President would obey an order
of the Supreme Court of the United States.

At this point I would like to juxtapose a few of the impeachment criteria
with some of the President's actions.

Impeachment criteria: James Madison, from the Virginia Ratification
Convention. "If the President be connected in any suspicious manner with
any person and there be grounds to believe that he will shelter him, he may
be impeached."

We have heard time and time again that the evidence reflects payment to
the defendants of money. The President had knowledge that these funds
were being paid and that these were funds collected for the 1972 Presidential campaign.

We know that the President met with Mr. Henry Petersen 27 times to
discuss matters related to Watergate and immediately thereafter met with
the very persons who were implicated in the information Mr. Petersen was
receiving and transmitting to the President. The words are, "if the President
be connected in any suspicious manner with any person and there be
grounds to believe that he will shelter that person, he may be impeached."

Justice Story: "Impeachment is intended for occasional and extraordinary
cases where a superior power acting for the whole people is put into operation to protect their rights and rescue their liberties from violations."

We know about the Huston plan. We know about the break-in of the psychiatrist's office. We know that there was absolute complete direction in
August 1971 when the President instructed Ehrlichman to "do whatever is
necessary." This instruction led to a surreptitious entry into Dr. Fielding's
office.

"Protect their rights." "Rescue their liberties from violation."

The South Carolina Ratification Convention impeachment criteria: Those
are impeachable "who behave amiss or betray their public trust."

Beginning shortly after the Watergate break-in and continuing to the present time the President has engaged in a series of public statements and
actions designed to thwart the lawful investigation by Government prosecutors. Moreover, the President has made public announcements and assertions bearing on the Watergate case which the evidence will show he
knew to be false.

These assertions, false assertions, impeachable, those who misbehave.
Those who "behave amiss or betray their public trust."

James Madison again at the Constitutional Convention: "A President is impeachable if he attempts to subvert the Constitution."

The Constitution charges the President with the task of taking care that the laws be faithfully executed, and yet the President has counseled his aides to commit perjury, willfully disregarded the secrecy of grand jury proceedings, concealed surreptitious entry, attempted to compromise a Federal judge while publicly displaying his cooperation with the processes of criminal justice.

"A President is impeachable if he attempts to subvert the Constitution."

If the impeachment provision in the Constitution of the United States will not reach the offenses charged here, then perhaps that 18th century Constitution should be abandoned to a 20th century paper shredder. Has the President committed offenses and planned and directed and acquiesced in a course of conduct which the Constitution will not tolerate? That is the question. We know that. We know the question. We should now forthwith proceed to answer the question. It is reason, and not passion, which must guide our deliberations, guide our debate, and guide our decision.

A very different sort of speech is that of Hungate. His tone was down-to-earth, and somehow it seemed right that he hailed from Missouri. Let me quote from the first third of his speech:

Mr. Chairman, it has been my privilege to serve on this committee for 10 years since I came to Congress, and never have I been prouder of this committee and of serving on it than I am during this period of its supreme testing.

For weeks, even months, we have studied evidence, heard witnesses, and debated the solemn question of impeachment. The time has come for decisions. Further delay is unjustifiable. The time-consuming task of impeachment must go forward.

Should Richard M. Nixon be found guilty of obstruction of justice? Yes.

Should Richard M. Nixon be found guilty of abusing the powers of his office? Yes.

Should Richard M. Nixon be found guilty of contempt and defiance of the Congress and the courts? Yes.

And on the last charge he is a repeated offender.

We hear a great deal today about the presumably grim consequences of impeachment—an endless public trial, a people divided, a Government paralyzed, a Nation disgraced. But suppose the House should decide not to impeach Mr. Nixon. This would have its consequenses, too—and they deserve careful examination.

For the refusal to impeach would be a decision as momentous as impeachment itself. It would and could be interpreted only as meaning that Congress does not think Mr. Nixon has done anything to warrant impeachment. It would alter the historic relationship of Presidential power to the constitutional system of accountability for the use of that power. Our message to posterity would be that Mr. Nixon had conceived and established a new conception of Presidential accountability, and his successors can expect to inherit Mr. Nixon's conception of inherent Presidential authority and wield the unshared power with which he will have endowed the Presidency. Failure to impeach would be a vindication of a new theory of Presidential nonaccountability.

Many would shrink from this trying constitutional responsibility. Shrinking from impeachment probably arises from the remoteness of contemporary Presidents, and from the difficulty of visualizing the offenses of his administration. Perhaps the situation is more easily conceived if put in terms more homely and local. A letter of Robert P. Weeks in the Ann Arbor News did this well, I think, and I would like to paraphrase it.

1. Suppose your mayor approved a plan by which the chief of your city's police department would illegally tap your phone, open your mail, and burglarize your apartment, your office, or your house;

2. Suppose your mayor directed your hometown police and FBI agents to tap the phone of your local reporter covering city hall; directed the FBI to investigate a newscaster for the local radio and TV station;

3. Suppose your mayor withheld knowledge of a burglary from a local judge trying a case in which that knowledge was important;

4. Suppose your mayor secretly taped conversations held in his office in your city hall between himself and citizens like yourself as well as public officials, then when a confirmed court order required him to turn over nine of these tapes, refused to obey; then, reversed himself; then announced that two of the tapes containing perhaps the most critically important material did not exist;

5. Suppose your mayor tripled his wealth while serving as mayor.

6. Suppose your mayor paid practically no income taxes for several years because he claimed huge and legally dubious deductions for turning over his official papers to the local historical society;

7. Suppose your mayor surreptitiously used your city's taxpayers' funds to make major improvements on two private homes he had;

8. Suppose your mayor twice selected personally as mayor pro tem a man who had bribes delivered to him in city hall and then resigned, allegedly to avoid going to jail;

9. Suppose your mayor selected and supervised as trusted top officials of his administration 10 men who were indicted, convicted or pleaded guilty—including the city attorney.

The citizens of your town would not be complacent. "Should we hold our city's elected officials to one high standard of conduct but have a much lower, more lax standard for the President? . . . Inaction would say to this President and future Presidents, "There's practically no limit to the improprieties we'll put up with in the White House."

During the course of debate, Hungate appointed himself to be the lawyer who represented all of the nonlawyers of the world. He was even so bold as to think that humor was appropriate. The following passage does not seem as funny now as it did at the time, and perhaps this is evidence of how high tension was. Everyone was on edge, so that even a feeble joke had an enormous power to break the tension (the bracketed additions are in the transcript):

I thank the chairman and I would like to begin by commending our colleague, Mr. Sarbanes, who seems to be the target for tonight, on a rather excellent job I think of explaining what he has worked out here and what is going on. This reminds me a great deal of an old saying of our former distinguished chairman, Mr. Celler, "I can give you explanations, I can't give you understanding."

I think Mr. Sarbanes has done an excellent job.

The impeachment grounds, as the chairman has indicated, indeed are quite broad. As I understand it, in the case of Andrew Johnson, they passed a resolution of impeachment, came back and drew up nine articles, went over in the Senate, decided they needed some more and drew a couple more. So going into all of this great, I hesitate to say specifically, I really can't say specificity—I didn't mean to say it.

[Laughter.]

As we get into all these legal terms, it is a lot of fun, for 38 lawyers, 38 good lawyers, I think—well—37 good lawyers. It is a lot of fun, but we forget perhaps that in the House of Representatives they aren't all lawyers and the public likes it that way, I think. They may like it better. As for strict standards of proof—I saw where one of the distinguished Senators said yesterday that some of them had differing views from the discussions we had about rules of evidence. The Senate will decide on the rules of evidence and as I recall in the *Johnson* case they did. They overruled the Supreme Court's

Chief Justice so many times that he finally threatened to quit and leave unless they behaved a little better.

So I think it is educational for us lawyers but the doctrine of impeachment, is as strong as the Constitution and as broad as the King's imagination, and we have that problem now, perhaps.

All the technicalities just remind me of the story of an old Missouri lawyer—the fellow was kind of a country fellow and got a case finally in the Supreme Court. He was nervous. He got up there and was arguing along and one of these judges looked down at him and he said, "Well, young man, where you come from do they ever talk the doctrine of 'qui facit per aluim facit per se?'"

Well, he said, "Judge, they hardly speak of anything else." [Laughter.]

Let me tell you I think Mr. Haldeman faked it per aluim and Mr. Ehrlichman faked it per aluim there is lots of evidence. If they don't understand what we are talking about now, they wouldn't know a hawk from a handsaw anyway.

Seriously, we know what we are discussing. It is really a question of pleading and I think we are seeking to—piling inference on inference. There you go again piling inferences.

We sit through these hearings day after day. I tell you, if a guy brought an elephant through that door and one of us said that is an elephant, some of the doubters would say, you know, that is an inference. That could be a mouse with a glandular condition. [Laughter.]

And perhaps one of them might be, but not 12, or even 28 volumes.

I have quoted Hungate at length because I think he touched the central problem. He paraphrased and quoted from a letter in which a citizen, Robert P. Weeks, constructed an extended analogy between a mayor and a president. Hungate understands that our problem is that we are afraid to judge a president in the way we judge a mayor. Consequently, Hungate thinks that it is important to insist that our ordinary ways of talking are fundamental, and thus he knows that humor is important. Unless we can see that certain arguments are ludicrous, and therefore should be laughed away, then we will not be able to meet the challenge of more demanding intellectual tasks. Unless we can recognize the ludicrous, we will not be able to distinguish the merely plausible from the sound. By leading his colleagues to laughter, Hungate reminded them that there is a difference between nonsense and sense.

As for the debate on Article I, it was primarily a factual debate: did the evidence support the charge? Those who defended Nixon denied that there was sufficient proof to show that he was involved in the cover-up. In making this argument, it was possible to get technical in various sorts of ways: one might voice a preference for direct evidence instead of circumstantial evidence; one could narrow the focus to particular acts instead of a broad pattern of action; one could be concerned with technical questions about the specificity of the charges and burdens of proof. Some, but not all, of those who defended the president made these arguments, although to argue in this way was to tend toward "the niceties of a narrow jurisprudence," and thus to depart from the spirit of Rodino's statement of question.

Some of the proponents leapt in and took up the burden of refuting these technical arguments. Those who did so might have had disparate reasons: some might have believed that the technicalities were relevant and thought that it was absolutely crucial to refute them; others might have been caught up in the passion for argument and sought to refute for the sake of refuting, even though they thought the point irrelevant; and some might have thought that the technical arguments would be politically effective and so engaged in refutation in an attempt to forestall embarrassment in the eyes of the public.

At any rate, whatever the reasons, refutations were offered. One of them went like this: It is true that the charges, as drafted, are not specific in the way that charges of impeachment were specific in the nineteenth-century precedents. However, pleadings in ordinary courts of law were different in the nineteenth century than they are today. Nowadays, one need only give notice of what the issues are going to be; in those days, one had to state the issue, being highly particular and using the artificial jargon of the law. We have changed, we believe that the change has improved the administration of justice; and judged by these changes, the matter is properly pleaded.

Consider another technical defense, that there was no direct evidence. The proponents of impeachment had a response: It is true that we don't have an admission by Nixon of guilt, and we don't have any witnesses who will say that they heard Nixon give a direct order to cover it up, and we don't have any witnesses who will say that they heard Nixon incriminate himself; but we have something that is just as good and that is direct evidence. The tapes contain Nixon's own words, and if you listen to them and give them a fair interpretation, then it is obvious that he knew what was happening and was in charge.

At this point, I must interrupt and wonder whether one ought to laugh or cry. First of all, it is hard to see why the distinction should matter; as some of the members themselves pointed out, it is a daily occurrence in our courts that crimes are declared and fortunes lost on the basis of circumstantial evidence. The important question ought to be the cogency of the proof, not its classification into scholastic categories. Fortunately, little time was spent on this debate. There are no modern authorities on the distinction; however, as I understand the ancient authorities, one should call the evidence of the tapes direct evidence.

Aside from the technicalities of classification (i.e., what we should call the evidence), the question of evidence was important. We ought not to impeach on the basis of a suspicion that something has gone wrong, and thus it was good that the thirty-eight debated the question. The only unease that one might have in reading the debate about the evidence is the one that is inevitable in all historical inquiries. When we inquire into past events, when we try to reconstruct who did what and why, we generally proceed somewhat uneasily, for we can never proceed with certainty. One response to uncertainty is to discipline the inquiry with professional standards, and so lawyers and historians have developed their own professional vocabulary, together with their own specialized ways of proceeding. In both professions the novice is expected to serve an apprenticeship; in both it is an article of faith that the seasoned veteran can make a balanced assessment of the facts in a way that is beyond the powers of either the novice or the laity. As citizens, we need not resent the claims of this faith, but we must be wary of its possible perversions.

The professional rituals of fact-finding can be perverted if they are used as a way to avoid the finding of any facts. In such cases the rituals are being used not to discipline one's engagement with the facts but to avoid such an engagement. When rituals become dead in this way, when there is a loss of nerve, then the whole enterprise has become pointless. Consequently, when we hear lawyers employ the technicalities of their profession in talking about facts, we can always wonder whether there is good faith or bad in the talking. We cannot expect lawyers, and as I have noted, all of the thirty-eight were lawyers, to talk like historians, for they were not trained in that craft. Instead, we expect them to talk like lawyers, to use the techniques of the lawyer's craft; but we also feel entitled to have them use their techniques to decide the case, and not to avoid deciding it. As for the members of the Judiciary Committee, they did vote, a majority thought that the essential facts had been proved, and so perhaps we need not be suspicious of their good faith. My own impression is that some talked technicalities in good faith and some in bad and that, overall, no harm was done.

And finally, what about the merits? Which side had the better of argument? This question is idle. On July 24, 1973, the committee members had before them certain evidence; they debated and voted; they finished on July 30, 1973. One could, I suppose, look at what they had before them and construct a scorecard, but it would be an idle act, for there is other evidence. On August 5, 1973, Nixon made public a transcript of tapes of conversations with Haldeman—the tapes that had been litigated up to the Supreme Court. The date of the conversations between Nixon and Haldeman was June 23, 1972, which was six days after the Watergate burglary. After this new evidence came out, those who had defended Nixon changed their position.

The defense collapsed because the theory on which it rested was destroyed. The defenders had admitted one key fact—there was a cover-up—but they had argued that Nixon didn't know about it. They argued that Nixon did not learn the truth until late March 1973, that he then took personal charge of the investigation, and that within a month he took vigorous action. But the disclosure of the new tapes wrecked that defense. The tapes showed that six days after the break-in, Haldeman proposed to Nixon that they should try to cut back the FBI investigation by having the CIA tell the FBI that it would endanger some CIA operations. Nixon approved this proposal. There was now no doubt that Nixon was guilty of an obstruction of justice.

9   A CRITIQUE

In the preceding chapters, I have presented the arguments that were made in the Judiciary Committee. It is now time to ask whether the committee members talked as they should have talked? Did they represent us well? If we look into their talk as into a mirror, do we see ourselves reflected clearly? From my own memory of the events, I am sure that there were many in those days who did approve, for I can remember reading and hearing sentences that contained conclusions like "the system worked" or "democracy has prevailed" or "the rule of law has been vindicated." I do not know if those who praised then, using those words, would still praise today and use the same words. Perhaps most of them would.

However, there are those who did not praise, and one of the most eminent is the famous linguist Noam Chomsky. He is contemptuous of the praise for our political system that journalists published in the aftermath of Nixon's resignation. In rather icy prose, he has argued that Nixon's real mistake was in his choice of victims. It is true, Chomsky agrees, that Nixon used evil methods against his adversaries, but Chomsky doesn't believe that he was up against impeachment for that reason. After all, similar methods have been used against those who represent racial minorities or who are political radicals, but the public officials who directed those illegalities were not punished. (And Chomsky offers documentation for these charges.) However, since Nixon attacked people with power, he made the mistake of attacking people who could defend themselves.

Presented in a short paragraph, as I have just given it, Chomsky's argument is resistant to response. First of all, his argument does depend upon an assessment of the facts, and one might not agree with his description. I do not want to argue this point, for it would lead me away from Watergate and into the topic of the FBI's illegal practices in attacking the Socialist Workers party or the Black Panther party, and I do not wish to wander that way. However, speaking for myself, I will say that the facts are (more or less) as he says they are. It is indeed the case the political activity that is radical, not orthodox, is likely to be met with police harassment (or worse).

However, given these facts—FBI illegality—one still must draw conclusions. Let me set out Chomsky's conclusions in his own words, so that we can examine them:

> Mitsou Ronat: . . . how do you interpret the Watergate affair, which has often been presented in France as the "triumph" of democracy?
>
> Noam Chomsky: To consider the Watergate affair as a triumph of democracy is an error, in my opinion. The real question raised was not: Did Nixon employ evil methods against his political adversaries? but rather: Who were the victims? The answer is clear. Nixon was condemned, not because he employed reprehensible methods in his political struggles, but because he made a mistake in the choice of adversaries against whom he turned these methods. *He attacked people with power.*
>
> The telephone taps? Such practices have existed for a long time. He had an "enemies list"? But nothing happened to those who were on that list. I was on that list, nothing happened to me. No, he simply made a mistake in his choice of enemies: he had on his list the chairman of IBM, senior government advisors, distinguished pundits of the press, highly placed supporters of the Democratic Party. He attacked the Washington Post, a major capitalist enterprise. And these powerful people defended themselves at once, as would be expected. Watergate? Men of power against men of power. [Emphasis in original]

My own thesis in this book has been that our representatives debated the question in terms of contrasting metaphors, breach of trust versus rule of law. Furthermore, I have argued that the rule-of-law metaphor generally prevailed. It follows, almost inexorably, that the metaphor of democracy was not the major theme of the debates; consequently, I would agree with Chomsky that we ought not to characterize what happened as a "triumph of democracy." Article IV, the Cambodian bombing, did raise the issue of democracy, but it was defeated. However, this conclusion raises further questions, and I would like to turn to them now.

One question goes to the relationship among democracy, the rule of law, and breach of trust. For example, one might ask whether democracy is better served by rule-of-law talk or breach-of-trust talk. Another question is whether the rule-of-law talk was sincere, or whether it was sheer hypocrisy. For example, is Chomsky right when he says that Nixon was not impeached because of the "evil methods" that he used against his adversaries? None of these questions are easy to answer, and so I must work up to them gradually.

Let us start by emphasizing the obvious: the procedures for deposing a president are complicated. At one level of description, it is true that Nixon was driven from office by "men of power." Given our constitutional scheme, no one else had authority to do so. If we want to measure their actions against the norms of democracy, perhaps we should ask whether the "men of power" acted in accordance with the wishes of those who lack power, or whether they acted on their own behalf. In other words, we can ask whether they acted in accordance with Lincoln's maxim, that is, whether their action was "of the people, by the people, for the people."

Interestingly enough, there were those who worked in the Nixon White House who saw the matter in the same way as Chomsky purports to see it. For example, John Dean has described how he was told to use the IRS against the (now defunct) magazine *Scanlon's Monthly*. Dean was frightened, so he asked Murray Chotiner for advice. As Dean reports it, their conversation went like this:

"[L]et me ask you this, Murray. You're a lawyer. Isn't it illegal and therefore crazy to use IRS to attack someone the President doesn't like?"

"Not so," he snorted. He stopped and retrieved the calm he rarely lost. "John, the President is the head of the executive branch of this damn government. If he wants his tax collectors to check into the affairs of anyone, it's his prerogative. I don't see anything illegal about it. It's the way the game is played. Do you think for a second that Lyndon Johnson was above using the IRS to harass those guys who were giving him a hard time on the war? No sir. Nor was Lyndon above using IRS against some good Republicans like Richard Nixon. I'll tell you he damn near ruined a few."

In other words, there were those who worked in the White House who saw the issue as being nothing more than "men of power against men of power." Were our representatives any better? One could defend them by trying to distinguish the police harassment of the Socialist Workers party and the Black Panther party. One could argue that Watergate was worse. The distinction would be that high-level illegality ("evil methods") is worse than low-level illegality; the FBI's illegalities do not threaten the rule of law in the way that a president's illegality does.

This defense is sound enough. Given the logic of the rule-of-law metaphor, it makes sense. However, I am not satisfied with this defense. First of all, the response begs the question of the appropriateness of the rule-of-law metaphor. And second, it is too simple a description of the facts. I think that the facts are more complicated than most people realize.

To start with the question of political dynamics, why should one believe that members of Congress were interested in defending those whom Nixon was attacking? If one examines the votes, and considers the political careers of those who voted to impeach, it seems clear enough to me that Chomsky's description is not quite right. Many of those who voted to impeach were altogether pleased that Nixon was attacking those whom he attacked. Consequently, it seems equally plausible, as a matter of political dynamics, to suppose that Nixon could have got away with attacking those whom he attacked, if only he had done it in a different way.

Furthermore, I have some reservations about Chomsky's technique of pitting ideals against practice. He aims to show that our ideals are inconsistent with our practice, and he does this by showing that our adherence to the ideal of the rule of law is less than total. He also shows that our deviations from this ideal are not random but predictable; our representatives are more likely to give the benefit of the rule of law to those who are powerful and orthodox than they are to those who are powerless and unorthodox. Surely he is right, but it does not follow that the talk about the rule of law is hypocrisy.

The more plausible account is that we believe in several inconsistent things: that those who have power are good; that the rule of law is good; that our enemies are bad; that decisive action against our enemies is good; and so forth. Here, in order to understand our own culture, one needs to remember such cultural icons as the private detective (*The Maltese Falcon*) or the gunslinger (*Shane*). One must also remember that the word "legalistic" is a pejorative word of abuse. In short, there are many things in our culture that are inconsistent with the rule of law.

Our inconsistency is not best described as one between an ideal and the actual practice but as one between several different practices (efficiency, strength, law), and so the problem is not the one that Chomsky seems to identify. Chomsky writes as though our practice is inconsistent with our preaching, whereas I would prefer to say that our preaching itself is inconsistent, and the explanation for this inconsistency is that we act inconsistently. Perhaps he might accept what I have written, and say that the question is which of the several inconsistent ideals is the "real" one, that is, the one we "really" believe. Yet it seems to me that one can only answer, so far as Watergate is concerned: all of it; the whole mess.

Were this another book, I would try to give some account of why our ideals are inconsistent, but I do not wish to turn too far away from the question of Watergate, that is, of choosing among these inconsistent ideals. If I were to take on this explanatory task, I would begin by discarding the dichotomy of ideal and practice that may (or may not) be presupposed in Chomsky's account. The ideals mentioned above—strength, efficiency, lawfulness—are not separate from practice but part of it. We honor the athlete and the warrior because we admire their performance, embodied in which are the practice (and ideal) of strength and courage. So too for the engineer, whose pursuit of the practice and the ideal of efficiency has given us the airplane and the computer. And finally, we can find lawfulness present in any practice in which people honor their promises, observe the customary way of doing things, and so forth. Consequently, as I have said, were I to argue the question at length, I would deny the relevance of the dichotomy of ideals and practices. It would follow that I would not expect to find hypocrisy. Instead I would expect to find inconsistent practices. Perhaps there are those who imagine that the pursuit of strength, efficiency, and lawfulness simultaneously is not inconsistent, that there is some invisible hand that will bring them into harmony. Unfortunately, I can't believe it, and so when I see actions in which the words seem out of phase with the deeds, I tend to suspect divided loyalties instead of hypocrisy.

Finally, Chomsky may have overlooked a key fact in the dynamics. In particular, we should not forget what the decisive event was—the public reaction to the "Saturday Night Massacre." The public revulsion to Nixon's firing of Cox, and to his forcing the resignations of Richardson and Ruckelshaus because they would not fire Cox, was extraordinarily massive. My own memory is that up until that event most members of Congress were trying to put off doing anything, but that the public outcry forced their hands. I would judge that the "men of power" were vacillating until the public pressure moved them off dead center, but I am not able to say exactly why the general public was so outraged. Part of the response could have been that Nixon was like a "loose cannon" and thus out of control. If we were to address the question of the Saturday Night Massacre with the vocabulary that has been the theme of this book, we would have many ways of talking about it. We could say that Nixon threatened the separation of powers; we could say that he had attacked the rule of law; and we could say that he had breached his trust by acting for his own private benefit instead of for the public benefit. My own suspicion is that the public reaction included some of each of these responses.

Indeed, it is my memory of this public reaction, and my sense of its complexity, that generates my major reservation in accepting Chomsky's thesis. He doubts that our representatives believed in the rule of law, since he doesn't believe that Nixon was impeached for the "evil methods" that he used; but I am in fear of the possibility that they believed in it far more than the rest of us do. What I fear is that the complexity of the public reaction was not fairly represented in the Judiciary Committee.

Even so, there is much that moves me in what Chomsky has said. What is profound and true about his critique is that it was provoked by the invocation of the word "democracy." The relationship in our culture between the social practices known as "the rule of law" and "democracy" has been the subject of a long debate; de Tocqueville got us started on this topic; and Chomsky is right in believing that this relationship is what ought to be at stake in our talk about Watergate. One way of addressing the topic is to ask whether our representatives, who in democratic theory are supposed to represent us, were in fact doing something that can be called representative when they employed the metaphors of the rule of law. I doubt it, and perhaps this is the point of Chomsky's critique; he might agree with me on the matter.

However, I would now like to turn away from Chomsky's critique and make my own critique. Before doing so, I wish to state two theses that constitute the starting point for my criticisms. First, I think it is clear that the dominant metaphor among the thirty-eight was the metaphor of the rule of law. It may be that they in fact understood the event through this metaphor, or it could be that they used it because they thought that it provided the best way to present their actions to us, for they may have thought that we could not accept impeachment in any other way. One can be uncertain about why they used this metaphor, but I am not uncertain about the fact that the rule-of-law metaphor was dominant.

My second thesis is that the use of this metaphor did not represent our views. As I have already said, in referring to the Saturday Night Massacre, I believe that the public response included that metaphor but also included much that cannot be subsumed under it.

And finally, there is the ultimate ethical question: how should we talk about Watergate?

10 CONCLUSION

When I have said in conversation some of the things that I have written in this book, I have noticed that some people don't believe me. Of course, there is no skepticism about my reading of the transcript. People believe me when I say that the transcript is dominated by the metaphor of the rule of law. Either they trust me as a reader or they have their own memory which fits well enough with my reading; so my first claim is accepted.

However, my second claim is what bothers people. How can I know whether the thirty-eight committee members were unrepresentative? Those who object see the public reaction as amorphous and without shape. If they are right, then I concede that it would make no sense to say that the thirty-eight were unrepresentative. On the contrary, one would have to say that the committee members had to be definite about matters on which the public was indefinite.

Alternatively, one can see public opinion as contradictory; there were divisions among us. Whenever there are divisions and contradictions of this sort, then the practical consequences, so far as politicians are concerned, are the same as those from an amorphous and chaotic public opinion. For a politician, that is, contradiction is the functional equivalent of chaos. We need not accept this as some general theoretical truth, but there is surely some justice in saying that as a practical matter, for a politician, it is a political truth. One might suppose that there would be a difference in that a politician can choose sides whenever there is division, something that cannot be done when there is chaos. However, it is possible to take sides only if the divisions are stable, and they generally aren't; to take an example that is removed from Watergate, antiinflationary policies can be popular when started and then turn out to be unpopular.

This critique of my second claim is factual: that I can't know what I need to know in order to compare public opinion with the words spoken in the Judiciary Committee. There is another critique of my second claim, and it is a moral one. In order to justify my assertion, I need to say what would be representative. This is really a claim that I could be more representative of the public than the thirty-eight committee members were, and this in turn is really a claim that I know how to talk about Watergate, that I know what should have been said. I confess that this is a powerful critique.

Indeed, I cannot establish my credentials: I don't know anything more about what the American people were thinking than anyone else does, and my moral authority is no more impressive than anyone else's. However, even if I can't prove anything, I am confident that my position is not eccentric. First of all, it is well established that the majority of our population is far less devoted to civil liberties and the rule of law than the elites are. For example, the sociologists who do surveys tell us that the blue-collar worker who is a union member is quite likely to be very liberal on economic issues, but not so on freedom-of-speech issues. From this I infer, with some risk, that most people (the majority, the masses) did *not* use the rule-of-law metaphor when they argued about Watergate and the impeaching of Richard Nixon. However, there is a good argument that this inference is as irrelevant as it is shaky.

One could grant that our representatives were not statistically representative of us and still not be swayed by that conclusion. Granting the statistical fact, one could still believe that the rule-of-law metaphor was the best way for them to have talked about Watergate. They did need a vocabulary that would sound nonpartisan, and the rule-of-law metaphor has the right sort of sound. Secondly, it gave them a way of distinguishing ordinary offenses from the sort of offenses that only a public official can commit, and one can argue that this is a good distinction. Thirdly, the metaphor gave them a way of grading the relative seriousness of different kinds of official misconduct; the use of the metaphor gave them ways to argue that some types of misconduct are more threatening to our system of government than others.

I must admit that there are no logical flaws in this sort of argument, that one can make it without being morally mistaken, and that adhering to it may be a prudent and reasonable social policy. I would insist that one who defends on this grounds must also face up to the dangers of the metaphor. One danger is that people start taking it literally, and so they become caught up in the words and lose their bearings. It is a fair reading of the transcript to say that this danger was not always avoided; sometimes the talk went astray. Furthermore, the metaphor of law can degenerate into legalism; and once again, anyone who reads the transcript can find some legalistic nonsense.

These are warnings that I would have to make to someone who defends the use of the rule-of-law metaphor. I would expect the defender to concede the merits of my warning, to acknowledge that the dangers were not hypothetical and in fact occurred, and yet to say that on balance the good things that were said outweighed the foolish. And I can understand how a defender might say these sorts of things; indeed, as I read I was struck by the subtlety and the creativity with which the metaphor was sometimes used. At times it was altogether obvious that the person speaking knew very well that the talk was metaphorical, knew well that legal words were being used to talk about something that was other than legal.

Even so, I have my regrets. The direction that I would have had the committee members take is toward the topic of self-government. There was talk about the nonlegal topics of democracy and self-government, but not often enough for my tastes. And when we look at the vote on the proposed Article IV, the Cambodia article, and when we see how Article III, the subpoena article, was first amended and then passed only narrowly, we can see that the topics of power, the structure of government, the theory of democracy, and citizen participation in government were topics with which the committee members felt uncomfortable. For me, this is regrettable.

Moreover, I think that this is not a purely personal or idiosyncratic regret. Indeed, I am willing to argue that it is why the thirty-eight were unrepresentative. To make this claim, I must offer a reading of our politics, and so I will risk an assertion: a constant theme of our politics for the past several decades has been a sense of frustration, and the source of that frustration, and its consequent politics of resentment, has been the feeling that we have lost all control over our lives and our government. This is a large topic and to follow it would take us in many directions, but it has a special relevance to impeachment in that the presidency is one of those things that is out of control. Being out of control, the presidency is alienated from us in ways that pose a fundamental danger to democracy.

So, in talking about Watergate, I would have had our representatives talk about this alienation. The problem is to develop metaphors that could be helpful and healthy in reviving democracy. No one, except for the most powerful of writers, can create good metaphors. This is not the sort of thing that can be a private act; it must be accepted by the community. So I shall not try to invent metaphors but shall borrow one that is already in use.

My own suggestion for an alternate metaphor is "breach of trust." The phrase has its roots in our legal system, but from that part of it known as "equity." Within the system of equity, the charge of a breach of trust is a charge that the trustee has not acted on behalf of the beneficiary of the trust as he or she should have. As a metaphor for politics, this idea has its possibilities. A trustee is supposed to act on behalf of another, and politicians are chosen to act as our representatives. Furthermore, trusting and being trusted are ordinary human experiences, and so the use of this metaphor would let us talk about politics in a language that could be connected with everyday life, whereas the rule-of-law metaphor is more formal. If the members of the Judiciary Committee used this metaphor, their talk might have been less technical and more colloquial, and the change would have been good. Furthermore, the ideal that was propounded could have been more human and less abstract, and I think this change too would have been good.

If we used the metaphor of trust to talk about Watergate, what would we say? We would not need to abandon the metaphors of law and the rule of law, but we would have to make the law a part of the larger equity of trust, and then make trust a part of the larger polity of democracy. We would have to abandon the notion that law can provide us with the standard of judgment or that law is a good in and of itself; but we would not have to abandon the notion that law is valuable, and we could find its value by knowing how it is part of trusting one another and being a democracy.

As with any metaphor, we cannot push this one too far; we must remember that it is a figure of speech. For example, we do not expect the trustee of an ordinary trust to go beyond the law and do things that are apparently illegal in executing the trust. The ordinary trustee is not expected to take such risks. However, a president sometimes is. As World War II was under way, but at a time when we were not yet engaged, President Franklin Delano Roosevelt employed our naval forces in the Atlantic so as to keep open the lanes of maritime commerce; this step was referred to as the "Naval War," and it was of doubtful legality. Furthermore, Roosevelt gave destroyers and other such equipment to the British in the program that was known as "Lend-Lease," and these acts seemed in direct contravention of a statute. But despite the apparent illegality of these acts, we do not think of them as a breach of his trust.

An even more extreme case is the wartime presidency of Abraham Lincoln. Measured by the norms of legality, his acts were unlawful. As James Randall summarizes the matter in the concluding chapter of his book *Constitutional Problems under Lincoln*, "He carried his executive authority to the extent of freeing the slaves by proclamation, setting up a whole scheme of state-making for the purpose of reconstruction, suspending the *habeas corpus* privilege, proclaiming martial law, enlarging the army and navy beyond the limits fixed by existing law, and spending public money without congressional appropriation." Randall is right in judging that these acts were illegal, if we use the ordinary standards of law to judge them. He knows that Lincoln is regarded "in popular conception as a great democrat, the exponent of liberty and of government by the people," and yet it also seems clear to him that Lincoln seized "more arbitrary power than perhaps any other President" in our history.

However, Lincoln did not abuse his trust, and although Randall does not use this metaphor, he says as much in other words. Randall carefully distinguishes the power Lincoln seized from the power he used, and thus, although Randall judges that he seized an arbitrary power, he acquits Lincoln altogether of having exercised that power in an arbitrary way. Lincoln himself was one reason: "His humane sympathy, his humor, his lawyerlike caution, his common sense, his fairness toward opponents, his dislike of arbitrary rule, his willingness to take the people into his confidence and to set forth patiently the reasons for unusual measures"—all these qualities distinguish a Lincoln from a Nixon. Using Randall's distinction, I could say that Nixon seized far less power but used it far more arbitrarily. More important, I would want to borrow Randall's description of Lincoln and use it to talk about trust.

Randall understands his description of Lincoln as an explanation of why his arbitrary power had a generally benign effect. Having made his description, Randall finishes his sentence: "—all these elements of his character operated to modify and soften the acts of overzealous subordinates and to lessen the effect of harsh measures upon individuals." In this passage Randall is giving us an explanation that is in a sense causal: a moderate person is likely to exercise power moderately, and the consequences are likely to be moderate. As an explanation, it seems plausible enough, and at any rate, whatever the merits of this explanatory scheme, it is true that the consequences were moderate. Randall's conclusion may not be satisfactorily explained by his premises, but his conclusion is nonetheless correct.

Take, for example, freedom of the press. As Randall describes it, the measures taken against the press included "the suppression of certain newspapers, the military control of the telegraph, the seizure of particular editions, the withholding of papers from the mails, and the arrest of editors." This is a rather formidable list, and yet these measures were not typical, and so Randall concludes: "There was no real censorship, and in the broad sense the press was unhampered though engaging in activities distinctly harmful to the Government." With respect to this particular example of a free press, I would put the case even more strongly than Randall. If we compare the Civil war with World War I, World War II, the cold war, Korea, and Vietnam, it is clear that there was more vigorous press opposition of government policy during the Civil War than during any of its successors. (Randall wrote in 1926, and he did compare the Civil War favorably with World War I on the issue of a free press.)

If we move beyond the question of a free press into larger issues, Randall's conclusions are still warranted. The following passage seems sound, even today:

The powers grasped by Lincoln caused him to be denounced as a "dictator." Yet civil liberties were not annihilated and no thoroughgoing dictatorship was established. There was nothing like a Napoleonic *coup d'état*. No undue advantage was taken of the emergency to force arbitrary rule upon the country or to promote personal ends. A comparison with European examples shows that Lincoln's government lacked many of the earmarks of dictatorial rule. His administration did not, as in some dictatorships, employ criminal violence to destroy its opponents and perpetuate its power. It is significant that Lincoln half expected to be defeated in 1864. The people were free to defeat him, if they chose, at the polls.

With all of this summary I can agree, but I would like to reinterpret it so as to connect it with my understanding of the nature of a public trust. In order to do so, I return to Randall's description of Lincoln. Randall referred to Lincoln's "humane sympathy, his humor," and so forth as "elements of his character." True enough, and a great deal depends upon how one understands the word "character," but I think that it is essential to understand that these are not mere qualities but ways of acting. A humane sympathy can only be displayed through action; and we know that Lincoln had a good sense of humor because he told a lot of funny jokes and he also laughed at himself.

Furthermore, if we consider Randall's description of the elements of Lincoln's character, we see that the actions to which it alludes are not private and personal in their scope. Randall thought that Lincoln's character was exemplified in "his fairness toward opponents, his dislike of arbitrary rule, his willingness to take the people into his confidence and to set forth patiently the reason for unusual measures." All of these are ways of acting politically, and it is hard to draw the line between these ways of acting politically and their political consequences. If you act fairly toward your political opponents, then what happens to them is fair. We don't get a fair act and then as a separate matter get fair consequences; they're the same thing.

In short, my interpretation of Randall's description is that I understand Lincoln's character as a set of public acts, and what is important about these acts is that they were public. The presidency is a public trust, and a public trust must be exercised publicly. Of course, Lincoln had his military and diplomatic secrets, but the openness of his administration is extraordinary when it is compared with modern government.

All this argument might be accepted, and yet the example of Lincoln could be judged irrelevant. Even granting that Lincoln is the classic case of an illegality made irrelevant by the more important categories of a breach of trust, one might still be troubled by the suggestion that we should use the metaphors of trust to judge a president. Lincoln was extraordinary, his situation was extraordinary, and so perhaps we can't use his example as a way of judging more ordinary presidents.

I agree; this objection is sound. And the reason that it is sound is that it surely does not follow, as a matter of either logic or prudence, that a principle that is good for judging extreme cases is a good one for judging ordinary cases. As a logician would put it, that which is sometimes true is not necessarily always true.

With this objection in mind, one could insist that the metaphor of the rule of law is the best way to judge most cases. I don't agree; I still prefer the notion of trust; but I do wish to recognize what is true in the claim for the richness of the rule-of-law metaphor.

The way to proceed in these matters is to find ways to unite the talk about law with the talk about the public trust and politics. There were those who argued for the exactly opposite road: they argued that politics should play no part because they believed that there was no practical distinction between the political and the partisan; they argued that breach of trust could not be a standard because they believed that there was no practical distinction between general principles of equity and an arbitrary subjectivity; and so they concluded that one must judge upon the law and solely upon the law. These arguments for relying upon the law presuppose that it can be something separate from politics and equity. Much philosophical ink has been spilled on this topic, and one can read tomes devoted to such questions as "How 'political' are our judges?" and "How 'legalistic' are our legislators?" Whatever the answer to these questions might be, as a matter of historical fact, I would propose an answer about what ought to be: judges and legislators (and also the executives) should imagine themselves to be cooperating with one another, and this because it seems fair to assume that both politics and law will be healthier if all of our public actors share some common purposes.

Perhaps such hopes are utopian, and indeed, I have my fears; but with regard to Watergate it is possible to unite law and equity and politics. To show that it is possible, I need only present an appropriate performance. As such a performance, let me offer the opening statement of Rep. M. Caldwell Butler, the representative from the Sixth Congressional District of Virginia. By a happy geographical accident, he was my representative; but on Thursday, July 25, 1974, the representation was more than geographical. On that day he spoke as follows:

Let me express first, Mr. Chairman, to you and the other members of this committee the high regard I have come to have for all.

While this has been a most distasteful experience for us all, I share great pride in the manner in which the membership of this committee with few exceptions has conducted itself in these deliberations. I want to express my personal appreciation to the staff for the monumental task which they have performed with such diligence over these months.

I also want to say that I regret the unfortunate misunderstanding which developed between Mr. Jenner and the minority members. We are indebted to him for bringing his great experience and talent to bear upon this investigation and for his hard work and fine presentation to us.

I am particularly proud of the fine work of my fellow townsman, Sam Garrison, who as minority counsel restored balance to the final work of our presentation, while professionally keeping a secret even to this moment his personal view of the evidence.

Likewise, I would like to express once more the pride that I share in the significant accomplishments of the administration of Richard Nixon. I have worked with him in every national campaign in which he has taken part and indeed there are those who believe I would not be here today if it were not for our joint effort in 1972. And I am deeply grateful for the many kindnesses and courtesies he has shown me over the years. I am not unmindful of the loyalty I owe him. I mention this, Mr. Chairman, so that you may be aware how distasteful this proceeding is for me as it must have been for every other member of this committee.

And one more thing: I have a word for my colleagues on this side of the aisle and to my Republican friends who may be listening and for my colleague from Indiana who is concerned about the effect impeachment will have for the Republican party.

For years we Republicans have campaigned against corruption and misconduct in the administration of the Government of the United States by the other party. Indeed in my first political experience in 1952, Trumanism was the vehicle that carried Dwight D. Eisenhower to the White House. And, somehow or other, we have found the circumstances to bring that issue before the American people in every national campaign.

But Watergate is our shame. Those things happened in the Republican administration while we had a Republican in the White House and every single person convicted to date has one way or the other owed allegiance to the Republican Party.

We cannot indulge ourselves the luxury of patronizing or excusing the misconduct of our own people. These things have happened in our house and it is our responsibility to do what we can to clear it up. It is we, not the Democrats, who must demonstrate that we are capable of enforcing the high standards we would set for them.

I agree with the sentiments often expressed today and yesterday that the Congress of the United States and each Member is indeed being tested at this moment, but the American people may also reasonably inquire of the Republican Party, "Do you really mean what you have said?"

My colleague, the gentleman from California, Mr. Wiggins, in his very able opening remarks of this morning, reminds us once more that we must measure the conduct of the President of the United States against the standards imposed by law, in which he is eminently correct.

I would like to share with you for a moment some observations I have with reference to these standards.

Impeachment and trial in the Senate is the process by which we determine whether or not the President of the United States has measured up to the standards of conduct which the American people are reasonably entitled to expect of him. The conduct which the American people are reasonably entitled to expect of the President of the United States is spelled out in part in our Constitution and in part in our statutes.

We are particularly grateful to our colleague from New York, Congressman Fish, for his exposition on the duties imposed upon the President of the United States by our Constitution.

It is my judgment also that the standard of conduct which the American people are reasonably entitled to expect of their President is established in part by experience and precedent. That is one reason why I am so concerned by what has been revealed to us by our investigation.

It will be remembered that only a few hours ago the gentleman from Iowa, Mr. Mayne, has argued that we should not impeach because of comparable misconduct in previous administrations.

There are frightening implications for the future of our country if we do not impeach the President of the United States. Because we will, by this impeachment proceeding, be establishing a standard of conduct for the President of the United States which will for all time be a matter of public record.

If we fail to impeach, we have condoned and left unpunished a course of conduct totally inconsistent with the reasonable expectations of the American people; we will have condoned and left unpunished a Presidential course of conduct designed to interfere with and obstruct the very process which he is sworn to uphold; and we will have condoned and left unpunished an abuse of power totally without justification. And we will have said to the American people: "These misdeeds are inconsequential and unimportant."

If at the conclusion of my remarks I have some time remaining, Mr. Chairman, I will endeavor to respond to, at least a part of, the earlier commentary on the evidence. But for the moment, I have two observations which must have a bearing on what this Congress shall eventually do.

The people of the United States are entitled to assume that their President is telling the truth. The pattern of misrepresentation and half-truths that emerges from our investigation reveals a Presidential policy cynically based on the premise that the truth itself is negotiable.

Consider the case of Richard Kleindienst, nominee for the Attorney General of the United States. The President had told him in unmistakable terms that he was not to appeal the ITT case, but before the Senate of the United States Mr. Kleindienst explicitly denied any effort by the President to influence him in this regard. The President, having knowledge of this, affirmed to the American people his continuing confidence in this man.

The record is replete with official Presidential misrepresentations of noninvolvement, and representations of investigations and reports never made, if indeed undertaken at all. There are two references to a Dean report that we have not seen.

Consider the case of Daniel Shorr. In a moment of euphoria on Air Force I, Presidential aides called upon the FBI to investigate this administration critic. Upon revelation, Presidential aides fabricated and the President affirmed that Shorr was being investigated for possible Federal appointment— nothing could be further from the truth.

Let me observe also that throughout the extensive transcripts made available to us of intimate Presidential conversation and discussion there is no real evidence of regret for what occurred, or remorse, or resolution to change and precious little reference to, or concern for constitutional responsibility or reflection upon the basic obligations of the Office of the Presidency.

In short, power appears to have corrupted. It is a sad chapter in American history, but I cannot condone what I have heard; I cannot excuse it, and I cannot and will not stand still for it.

This is not to suggest that there are not many areas of our investigation which clearly reveal to me that some charges do not elevate themselves to this status of an impeachable offense. I am satisfied that the Presidential misrepresentations with reference to the Cambodian war is excusable because of the congressional and Security Council involvement in the decisionmaking itself. The impoundment of funds by the Office of the President is clearly an exercise of administrative discretion, which is now sharply curtailed by the Congress itself. While the manipulation of the decision to raise milk price supports by the President's advisers in order to reaffirm the pledge of substantial campaign contributions is reprehensible and bordering on bribery by itself, the evidence as to the President's direct involvement has nowhere been established to the extent, in my judgment, to warrant a charge of impeachment.

While I am seriously concerned about the manipulations of the deed of gift of Vice Presidential papers to the United States, I have real reservations as to whether the degree of Presidential involvement makes him guilty of an impeachable tax fraud.

But I do want to associate myself with the remarks of the gentleman from Illinois, Mr. Railsback, and others and particularly the careful manner in which he reviewed the President's response to the information which came to him in his official capacity, and his participation in the continuing policy of coverup, at least after the 21st day of March 1973. This is clearly a policy of obstruction of justice which cannot go unnoticed.

Likewise, I am concerned about the pattern of Presidential abuse of the power given him by statute and the Constitution. The manipulation of the Federal Bureau of Investigation, the Central Intelligence Agency, the Internal Revenue Service, and indeed the existence of the White House plumbers are frightening in their implications for the future of America.

The misuse of power is the very essence of tyranny.

The evidence is clear, direct, and convincing to me that the President of the United States condoned and encouraged the use of the Internal Revenue Service taxpayer audit as a means of harassing the President's political enemies.

And consider, if you will, the frightening implications of that for a free society.

Mr. Chairman, while I still reserve my final judgment, I would be less than candid if I did not now say that my present inclination is to support articles incorporating my view of the charges of obstruction of justice and abuse of power; but there will be no joy in it for me.

Let me say what I think is exemplary about this speech. Butler begins, following the custom in all of the speeches, with courtesies—with praise for the chairman, the staff, and his colleagues. As he turns to the merits, he starts on a personal note: campaigning against "corruption and misconduct" has been a standard theme for Republicans, including Butler himself: "Indeed in my first political experience in 1952, Trumanism was the vehicle that carried Dwight D. Eisenhower to the White House." Furthermore, this issue of corruption was not merely the battle flag of his youth, for "somehow or other, we have found the circumstances to bring that issue before the American people in every national campaign."

These words could have been spoken by a Democrat, but they would then have been a reproach; coming from a Republican, they are a self-imposed standard. "But Watergate is our shame. Those things happened in the Republican administration while we had a Republican in the White House and every single person convicted to date has one way or the other owed allegiance to the Republican Party." These two observations—that the Republicans have campaigned against corruption, but are now knee-deep in it—could be used in several ways, but Butler uses them to propose a citizen's hypothetical question: "the American people may . . . reasonably inquire of the Republican Party, 'Do you really mean what you have said?'"

These words are a truly admirable beginning. He is proposing to stand by what he has always claimed to stand by. A political promise is not a legally enforceable contract, and campaign promises are among the more suspect members of the genre. Even so, there are limits; the practice of politics demands that there be limits. Sooner or later, one must stand for something, or politics itself is impossible; otherwise, the voters can have no basis for voting.

This way of talking about politics is an ancient one. If one has reference to the words of those in England who struggled with the problem of executive power, one finds that they spoke of the social compact between the chief executive and the common man, and they made the claim that one can find limits to the executive power in this compact. These English polemicists were not referring to the philosopher's contract, the hypothetical agreement that moved us from the state of nature to civil society. Instead they had in mind the actual historical promises that kings had made, in their coronation oaths and in such documents as Magna Carta.

At any rate, Butler is able to state the ultimate question as being "whether or not the President of the United States has measured up to the standards of conduct which the American people are reasonably entitled to expect of him." And it seems to me that this reference to the reasonable expectations of the people follows nicely from what Butler has already said. But the problem is how to spell out the details, so that there can be some adequately practical way of making judgments. Unless there is to be some mysterious divination of the popular will, it would be nice to have sources that we can use as evidence for what the reasonable expectations might be. We cannot ask for certainty, or for clear rules, but we are entitled to know how one should argue.

Butler offers four sources that we can consult: the Constitution, statutes, experience, and precedent. Needless to say, such sources can be interpreted in various ways, and so we should consider how Butler is going to interpret them. Because his speech is brief, there being only fifteen minutes allotted to it, I must speculate a bit. I would begin by observing that all four of the items that Butler lists are public acts, and so his claim seems to be that our public acts are the things that have created expectations. In retrospect, this makes his earlier reference to campaign promises take on a new meaning; the regular pattern of campaigning that has been part of his career is transformed into a public act, a precedent.

There are also other clues that can help us understand what Butler means by the words "experience" and "precedent." One way to understand these words is to notice how he combines them with other words. Consequently, it seems important to me that immediately after Butler lists precedent as a source for standards, he turns to what has been said by "the gentleman from Iowa, Mr. Mayne, [who] has argued that we should not impeach because of comparable misconduct in previous administrations." Butler responds by saying that this argument has "frightening implications," since a failure to impeach will set a precedent by which Congress would be saying that what Nixon has done is "inconsequential and unimportant." Butler insists that if the Congress does nothing, then "we will have condoned and left unpunished an abuse of power totally without justification."

It is clear from this language that precedent is not being understood as a narrowly legal concept. For one thing, strong language is used, but perhaps that is not much of a clue, for lawyers can and do sometimes speak strongly about their precedents. Rather more important than the tone of Butler's rhetoric is the implied social context, and I mean by this odd phrase (the implied context) that Butler makes a larger than legal assertion about the use and meaning of precedent.

In the legal context, a precedent is a decision by a court that is used by a later court to help it decide a case. However, Butler is here talking about a precedent as something that establishes cultural meaning. He insists that if the Congress does not impeach, "we will have said to the American people" that what has happened does not really matter. This is a claim that precedent is a way of speaking, and thus an act that generates meaning.

If these few paragraphs are reliable clues for understanding Butler's words, for knowing how it is that our Constitution, statutes, experience, and precedents might be used to spell out standards of conduct, then of course it should be no surprise to read the principles that he can derive from the sources. His first principle is as follows: "The people of the United States are entitled to assume that their President is telling the truth." Judged by this standard, it is clear enough that Nixon can be found wanting, and Butler cites some examples.

His second standard of that which is a reasonable expectation is not stated directly but is instead offered implicitly by way of an observation. Butler notes that the committee members have read the transcripts of the tapes and that "there is no real evidence of regret for what occurred, or remorse, or resolution to change and precious little reference to, or concern for constitutional responsibility or reflection upon the basis obligations of the Office of the Presidency." This is a more complex evaluation than that of lying, but it is related to it, in that the charge is one of untruth to the claims of the office.

When someone speaks as Butler has done, he creates a special sort of contract with the reader. His topic is the reasonable expectations that we might have of the president, but in speaking this way he also generates some reasonable expectations about himself. He talks about the role of truth, and it is a truth not just of speaking but of acting in the execution of an office. Having made this his topic, we now expect him to perform truthfully the role of one who is considering impeachment. Consequently, as he turns to the specific charges and announces his position on each, we have expectations.

Even so, our expectations must be reasonable; as noted, each of the committee members had only fifteen minutes to speak, and Butler has at this point used up about three-fourths of his time. Given this constraint, he must move crisply through the charges. Unfortunately, his comments seem more than crisp; they seem cryptic. On first reading, they strike one as a set of conclusions that come without justification; and they seem disappointing. Indeed, I am sure that anyone who read the last quarter of Butler's speech, in isolation from what went before, would regard it as totally unremarkable.

He begins by ticking off the charges that he will not support: the Cambodian bombing article, "because of the Congressional and Security Council involvement in the decisionmaking itself"; and the tax-fraud accusation, because he is not sure about "the degree of Presidential involvement" in the wrongful acts. He also responds negatively to two charges that I have not discussed because they were never submitted to a vote. One of them, arising from Nixon's refusal to spend some of the money appropriated by Congress, has been dealt with by statute, and therefore Butler concludes that impeachment is not appropriate. The other has arisen from Nixon's decision to raise the price supports for milk, and the question is whether it was an unlawful response to a bribe; like the rest of the committee, Butler thinks that the charge has not been proved.

Having stated what he will not support, he moves to the charges that he finds justified. "But I do want to associate myself with the gentleman from Illinois, Mr. Railsback," about the cover-up charges of Article I. Butler's comment is brief, and it is interesting that he chooses to praise "the careful manner in which he [Railsback] reviewed the President's response to the information which came to him in his official capacity." Butler then speaks directly to the charge of abuse of power. At first his rhetoric is low-keyed; he says that he is "concerned." But his words quickly become more charged. He describes what the president has done as "manipulation" of such established agencies as the FBI, and he refers to manipulations of this sort and to the president's creation of a secret investigative agency within his staff as "frightening in their implications for the future of America."

He concludes by stating what he thinks these implications are— "The misuse of power is the very essence of tyranny"—and by picking out one specific incident: "The evidence is clear, direct, and convincing to me that the President of the United States condoned and encouraged the use of the Internal Revenue Service taxpayer audit as a means of harassing the President's political enemies." He returns to the implications: "And consider, if you will, the frightening implications of that for a free society."

His final sentence is: "Mr. Chairman, while I still reserve my final judgment, I would be less than candid if I did not now say that my present inclination is to support articles incorporating my view of the charges of obstruction of justice and abuse of power; but there will be no joy in it for me."

The most admirable thing about the performance is that Caldwell Butler takes a position on everything; he is not evasive. To be sure, he does not talk about the subpoena question, but the decision to present it as a separate charge has not yet been made at this point. The reasons that he gives for his no votes are not the sort that stir the heart; for the most part, he bases a vote of no on lack of "evidence" of the necessary degree of "involvement." In other speeches these words have a technical and legalistic sound, and they are used to narrow the issue. In this speech, with its emphasis on truth, the tonality of the emphasis on evidence is not technical. Instead, it is one way for Butler to be devoted to the truth; and so it is appropriate that Butler should single out for praise "the careful manner" in which Railsback has "reviewed" the evidence that Nixon has participated in an obstruction of justice. Being concerned about evidence is indeed one way of being truthful.

Even more important is the way Butler ends. The end of a speech is the place of emphasis, the place where one puts that which is most important, and so it is important that he ends with the charge of abuse of power. As I puzzle over these words, what strikes me as most significant is the relationship between law and politics that seems to be presupposed in Butler's finale. The particular abuses of power that he discusses all have to do with law enforcement, but he relates them to "tyranny" and to our future as "a free society." You may recall that in an earlier part of his speech, Butler says that our "statutes" are one of the sources that we can draw upon to spell out the details of the people's "reasonable expectations" of their president. Consequently, it strikes me as significant that each of the abuses that Butler lists is also beyond the president's statutory authority, even if it is not technically criminal. (Nixon's setting up of a secret investigative unit in his office is a clear example of this point.)

In other speeches I interpret this relationship differently, but here I think that it is fair to say that Butler understands the statutes of the United States to be a promise, just as his repeated campaigning against corruption is presented as a promise. These are all public acts that have a meaning, and about all of them the people are entitled to ask: "Do you really mean what you have said?"

Butler's speech is exemplary, for it shows us how to reunite the metaphors of law, politics, and trust. In Butler's discourse, making laws is like making promises, in that both generate public expectations; the politicians who speak with statutes and promises so as to generate these expectations have set the terms of their political trust, and we are entitled to hold them to what they have said. My own interpretation of Butler's words is that he has succeeded in making both law and politics into a subset of something larger, and that something is the idea of trust.

Needless to say, this way of talking is only a possibility, not a necessity. If we are offered it as a possibility, then we are left with a decision: would we wish to talk this way? Of course, one cannot decide these questions unilaterally and singly. Words can only have meaning in a community of speakers. And so we are left with a puzzle: could the metaphors of trust be the right ones for us?

APPENDIX

Report of the Committee on the Judiciary, House of Representatives:

The Committee on the Judiciary, to whom was referred the consideration of recommendations concerning the exercise of the constitutional power to impeach Richard M. Nixon, President of the United States, having considered the same, reports thereon pursuant to H. Res. 803 as follows and recommends that the House exercise its constitutional power to impeach Richard M. Nixon, President of the United States, and that articles of impeachment be exhibited to the Senate as follows:

RESOLUTION

Impeaching Richard M. Nixon, President of the United States, of high crimes and misdemeanors.

Resolved, That Richard M. Nixon, President of the United States, is impeached for high crimes and misdemeanors, and that the following articles of impeachment be exhibited to the Senate:

Articles of impeachment exhibited by the House of Representatives of the United States of America in the name of itself and of all of the people of the United States of America, against Richard M. Nixon, President of the United States of America, in maintenance and support of its impeachment against him for high crimes and misdemeanors.

Article I

In his conduct of the office of President of the United States, Richard M. Nixon, in violation of his constitutional oath faithfully to execute the office of President of the United States and, to the best of his ability, preserve, protect, and defend the Constitution of the United States, and in violation of his constitutional duty to take care that the laws be faithfully executed, has prevented, obstructed, and impeded the administration of justice, in that:

On June 17, 1972, and prior thereto, agents of the Committee for the Re-election of the President committed unlawful entry of the headquarters of the Democratic National Committee in Washington, District of Columbia, for the purpose of securing political intelligence. Subsequent thereto, Richard M. Nixon, using the powers of his high office, engaged personally and through his subordinates and agents, in a course of conduct or plan designed to delay, impede, and obstruct the investigation of such unlawful entry; to cover up, conceal and protect those responsible; and to conceal the existence and scope of other unlawful covert activities.

The means used to implement this course of conduct or plan included one of more of the following:

(1) making or causing to be made false or misleading statements to lawfully authorized investigative officers and employees of the United States;

(2) withholding relevant and material evidence or information from lawfully authorized investigative officers and employees of the United States;

(3) approving, condoning, acquiescing in, and counseling witnesses with respect to the giving of false or misleading statements to lawfully authorized investigative officers and employees of the United States and false or misleading testimony in duly instituted judicial and congressional proceedings;

(4) interfering or endeavoring to interfere with the conduct of investigations by the Department of Justice of the United States, the Federal Bureau of Investigation, the Office of Watergate Special Prosecution Force, and Congressional Committees;

(5) approving, condoning, and acquiescing in, the surreptitious payment of substantial sums of money for the purpose of obtaining the silence or influencing the testimony of witnesses, potential witnesses or individuals who participated in such unlawful entry and other illegal activities;

(6) endeavoring to misuse the Central Intelligence Agency, an agency of the United States;

(7) disseminating information received from officers of the Department of Justice of the United States to subjects of investigations conducted by lawfully authorized investigative officers and employees of the United States, for the purpose of aiding and assisting such subjects in their attempts to avoid criminal liability;

(8) making false or misleading public statements for the purpose of deceiv-

ing the people of the United States into believing that a thorough and complete investigation had been conducted with respect to allegations of misconduct on the part of personnel of the executive branch of the United States and personnel of the Committee for the Re-election of the President, and that there was no involvement of such personnel in such misconduct; or

(9) endeavoring to cause prospective defendants, and individuals duly tried and convicted, to expect favored treatment and consideration in return for their silence or false testimony, or rewarding individuals for their silence or false testimony.

In all of this, Richard M. Nixon has acted in a manner contrary to his trust as President and subversive of constitutional government, to the great prejudice of the cause of law and justice and to the manifest injury of the people of the United States.

Wherefore Richard M. Nixon, by such conduct, warrants impeachment and trial, and removal from office.

Article II

Using the powers of the office of President of the United States, Richard M. Nixon, in violation of his constitutional oath faithfully to execute the office of President of the United States and, to the best of his ability, preserve, protect, and defend the Constitution of the United States, and in disregard of his constitutional duty to take care that the laws be faithfully executed, has repeatedly engaged in conduct violating the constitutional rights of citizens, impairing the due and proper administration of justice and the conduct of lawful inquiries, or contravening the laws governing agencies of the executive branch and the purposes of these agencies.

This conduct has included one or more of the following:

(1) He has, acting personally and through his subordinates and agents, endeavored to obtain from the Internal Revenue Service, in violation of the constitutional rights of citizens, confidential information contained in income tax returns for purposes not authorized by law, and to cause, in violation of the constitutional rights of citizens, income tax audits or other income tax investigations to be initiated or conducted in a discriminatory manner.

(2) He misused the Federal Bureau of Investigation, the Secret Service, and other executive personnel, in violation or disregard of the constitutional rights of citizens, by directing or authorizing such agencies or personnel to conduct or continue electronic surveillance or other investigations for purposes unrelated to national security, the enforcement of laws, or any other

lawful function of his office; he did direct, authorize, or permit the use of information obtained thereby for purposes unrelated to national security, the enforcement of laws, or any other lawful function of his office; and he did direct the concealment of certain records made by the Federal Bureau of Investigation of electronic surveillance.

(3) He has, acting personally and through his subordinates and agents, in violation or disregard of the constitutional rights of citizens, authorized and permitted to be maintained a secret investigative unit within the office of the President, financed in part with money derived from campaign contributions, which unlawfully utilized the resources of the Central Intelligence Agency, engaged in covert and unlawful activities, and attempted to prejudice the constitutional right of an accused to a fair trial.

(4) He has failed to take care that the laws were faithfully executed by failing to act when he knew or had reason to know that his close subordinates endeavored to impede and frustrate lawful inquiries by duly constituted executive, judicial, and legislative entities concerning the unlawful entry into the headquarters of the Democratic National Committee, and the cover-up thereof, and concerning other unlawful activities, including those relating to the confirmation of Richard Kleindienst as Attorney General of the United States, the electronic surveillance of private citizens, the break-in into the office of Dr. Lewis Fielding, and the campaign financing practices of the Committee to Re-elect the President.

(5) In disregard of the rule of law, he knowingly misused the executive power by interfering with agencies of the executive branch, including the Federal Bureau of Investigation, the Criminal Division, and the Office of Watergate Special Prosecution Force, of the Department of Justice, and the Central Intelligence Agency, in violation of his duty to take care that the laws be faithfully executed.

In all of this, Richard M. Nixon has acted in a manner contrary to his trust as President and subversive of constitutional government, to the great prejudice of the cause of law and justice and to the manifest injury of the people of the United States.

Wherefore Richard M. Nixon, by such conduct, warrants impeachment and trial, and removal from office.

Article III

In his conduct of the office of President of the United States, Richard M. Nixon, contrary to his oath faithfully to execute the office of President of the United States and, to the best of his ability, preserve, protect, and defend the Constitution of the United States, and in violation of his constitutional duty to take care that the laws be faithfully executed, has failed without lawful cause or excuse to produce papers and things as directed by duly authorized subpoenas issued by the Committee on the Judiciary of the House of Representatives on April 11, 1974, May 15, 1974, May 30, 1974, and June 24, 1974, and willfully disobeyed such subpoenas. The subpoenaed papers and things were deemed necessary by the Committee in order to resolve by direct evidence fundamental, factual questions relating to Presidential direction, knowledge, or approval of actions demonstrated by other evidence to be substantial grounds for impeachment of the President. In refusing to produce these papers and things, Richard M. Nixon, substituting his judgment as to what materials were necessary for the inquiry, interposed the powers of the Presidency against the lawful subpoenas of the House of Representatives, thereby assuming to himself functions and judgments necessary to the exercise of the sole power of impeachment vested by the Constitution in the House of Representatives.

In all of this, Richard M. Nixon has acted in a manner contrary to his trust as President and subversive of constitutional government, to the great prejudice of the cause of law and justice, and to the manifest injury of the people of the United States.

Wherefore Richard M. Nixon, by such conduct, warrants impeachment and trial, and removal from office.

The following two articles were rejected.

In his conduct of the office of President of the United States, Richard M. Nixon, in violation of his oath faithfully to execute the office of President of the United States and, to the best of his ability, preserve, protect, and defend the Constitution of the United States, and in disregard of his constitutional duty to take care that the laws be faithfully executed, on and subsequent to March 17, 1969, authorized, ordered, and ratified the concealment from the Congress of the facts and the submission to the Congress of false and misleading statements concerning the existence, scope and nature of American bombing operations in Cambodia in derogation of the power of the Congress to declare war, to make appropriations and to raise and support armies, and by such conduct warrants impeachment and trial and removal from office.

In his conduct of the office of President of the United States, Richard M. Nixon, in violation of his constitutional oath faithfully to execute the office of the President of the United States, and, to the best of his ability, preserve, protect and defend the Constitution of the United States, and in violation of his constitutional duty to take care that the laws be faithfully executed, did receive emoluments from the United States in excess of the compensation provided by law pursuant to Article II, Section 1, of the Constitution, and did willfully attempt to evade the payment of a portion of Federal income taxes due and owing by him for the years 1969, 1970, 1971, and 1972, in that:

(1) He, during the period for which he has been elected President, unlawfully received compensation in the form of government expenditures at and on his privately-owned properties located in or near San Clemente, California, and Key Biscayne, Florida.

(2) He knowingly and fraudulently failed to report certain income and claimed deductions in the years 1969, 1970, 1971, and 1972 on his Federal income tax returns which were not authorized by law, including deductions for a gift of papers to the United States valued at approximately $576,000.

In all of this, Richard M. Nixon has acted in a manner contrary to his trust as President and subversive of constitutional government, to the great prejudice of the cause of law and justice and to the manifest injury of the people of the United States.

NOTES

Chapter 1. The Question

In the second paragraph of this chapter, I state the theoretical thesis on which the book rests, that is, that descriptions about Watergate tell us more about the person speaking than about the event described. There are numerous authorities that I could cite for this sort of thesis, and I could implead these authorities from many places in the academy; however, I prefer to rest my thesis on the testimony of literature.

Jane Austen's *Pride and Prejudice*, chapter 13, has the example that I want. The scene opens with Mr. Bennet, his wife, and his five daughters seated at the breakfast table; Mr. Bennet announces that they are having a guest for dinner. They question him, he toys with their questions, but finally tells them that his cousin, Mr. Collins, will be their guest. The problem that lies behind this visit is that the house in which the Bennets live is "entailed" by way of the complicated devices that were then part of English property law. The arrangement was a threat to the security of the Bennet family: the land was to go to Mr. Collins on Mr. Bennet's death, and the widow and daughters could be dispossessed.

The visit has been announced in a letter which Mr. Bennet has received some time before but which he now reveals to the family for the first time. When the members of the family respond to the letter, each of them does so in a way that tells us more about her character than about the content of the letter. The event is presented in the following excerpt:

"About a month ago I received this letter, and about a fortnight ago I answered it, for I thought it a case of some delicacy, and required early attention. It is from my cousin, Mr. Collins, who, when I am dead, may turn you all out of this house as soon as he pleases."

"Oh! my dear," cried his wife, "I cannot bear to hear that mentioned. Pray do not talk of that odious man. I do think it is the hardest thing in the world, that your estate should be entailed away from your own children; and I am sure if I had been you, I should have tried long ago to do something or other about it."

Jane and Elizabeth attempted to explain to her the nature of an entail. They had often attempted it before, but it was a subject on which Mrs Bennet was beyond the reach of reason; and she continued to rail bitterly against the cruelty of settling an estate away from a family of five daughters, in favour of a man whom nobody cared anything about.

"It certainly is a most iniquitous affair," said Mr Bennet, "and nothing can clear Mr Collins from the guilt of inheriting Longbourn. But if you will listen to his letter, you may perhaps be a little softened by his manner of expressing himself."

"No, that I am sure I shall not; and I think it was very impertinent of him to write to you at all, and very hypocritical. I hate such false friends. Why could not he keep on quarrelling with you, as his father did before him?"

"Why, indeed, he does seem to have had some filial scruples on that head, as you will hear."

Hunsford, near Westerham, Kent.
15th October.

Dear Sir,

The disagreement subsisting between yourself and my late honoured Father, always gave me much uneasiness, and since I have had the misfortune to lose him, I have frequently wished to heal the breach; but for some time I was kept back by my own doubts, fearing lest it might seem disrespectful to his memory for me to be on good terms with any one, with whom it had always pleased him to be at variance.—'There, Mrs Bennet.'—My mind however is now made up on the subject, for having received ordination at Easter, I have been so fortunate as to be distinguished by the patronage of the Right Honorable Lady Catherine de Bourgh, widow of Sir Lewis de Bourgh, whose bounty and beneficence has preferred me to the valuable rectory of this parish, where it shall be my earnest endeavour to demean myself with grateful respect toward her Ladyship, and be ever ready to perform those rites and ceremonies which are instituted by the Church of England. As a clergyman, moreover, I feel it my duty to promote and establish the blessing of peace in all families within the reach of my influence; and on these grounds I flatter myself that my present overtures of goodwill are highly commendable, and that the circumstance of my being next in the entail of Longbourn estate, will be kindly overlooked on your side, and not lead you to reject the offered olive branch. I cannot be otherwise than concerned at being the means of injuring your amiable daughters, and beg leave to apoligise for it, as well as to assure you of my readiness to make them every possible amends,—but of this hereafter. If you should have no objection to receive me into your house, I propose myself the satisfaction of waiting on you and your family, Monday, November 18th, by four o'clock, and shall probably trespass on your hospitality till the Saturday se'night following, which I can do without any inconvenience, as Lady Catherine is far from objecting to my occasional absence on a Sunday, provided that some other clergyman is engaged to do the duty of the day. I remain, dear sir, with respectful compliments to your lady and daughters, your well-wisher and friend,

William Collins

"At four o'clock, therefore, we may expect this peace-making gentleman," said Mr Bennet, as he folded up the letter. "He seems to be a most conscientious and polite young man, upon my word; and I doubt not will prove a valuable acquaintance, especially if Lady Catherine should be so indulgent as to let him come to us again."

"There is some sense in what he says about the girls however; and if he is disposed to make them any amends, I shall not be the person to discourage him."

"Though it is difficult," said Jane, "to guess in what way he can mean to make us the atonement he thinks our due, the wish is certainly to his credit."

Elizabeth was chiefly struck with his extraordinary deference for Lady Catherine, and his kind intention of christening, marrying, and burying his parishioners whenever it were required.

"He must be an oddity, I think," she said. "I cannot make him out.—There is something very pompous in his stile.—And what can he mean by apologizing for being next in the entail?—We cannot suppose he would help it, if he could.—Can he be a sensible man, sir?"

"No, my dear; I think not. I have great hopes of finding him quite the reverse. There is a mixture of servility and self-importance in his letter, which promises well. I am impatient to see him."

"In point of composition," said Mary, "his letter does not seem defective. The idea of the olive branch is not wholly new, yet I think it is well expressed."

To Catherine and Lydia, neither the letter nor its writer were in any degree interesting. It was next to impossible that their cousin should come in a scarlet coat, and it was now some weeks since they had received pleasure from the society of a man in any other colour. As for their mother, Mr Collins's letter had done away much of her ill-will, and she was preparing to see him with a degree of composure, which astonished her husband and daughters.

As I said above, there are other authorities, but I am one of those who consider the divine Jane authority enough.

The quotation from Edmund Burke is taken from his *Reflections on the Revolution in France* (1790). In the Penguin edition (1970), edited by Coner Cruise O'Brien, it appears at p. 183.

Chapter 2. Chronology

The most useful source for a chronology of the Watergate affair is the Congressional Quarterly, Inc., *Watergate: Chronology of a Crisis* (Washington, D.C., 1975), which presents events in the order in which they were made public. The quotations from Ehrlichman and Kleindienst that appear in the middle of the chapter are taken from this source, pp. 240 and 37, respectively.

The quotation from Woodward and Bernstein is from *All the President's Men* (New York, 1974), p. 19. The quotation from John Mitchell, the director of CREEP, appears in the same book at p. 20.

Anyone who wishes to investigate the political dynamics of the Watergate affair needs to start with the way the news was presented in the press. In addition to the two sources cited above, one should consult Barry Sussman's *The Great Cover-up: Nixon and the Scandal of Watergate* (New York, 1974); Sussman was the editor who supervised Woodward and Bernstein, and so his perspective on events is especially valuable. Many other journalists wrote about the affair, but two short books which are especially interesting in giving the flavor of events are Mary McCarthy's *The Mask of State: Watergate Portraits* (New York, 1974) and Jimmy Breslin's *How the Good Guys Finally Won* (New York, 1975). A journalist's account of the operations of the House Judiciary Committee is Howard Fields's *High Crimes and Misdemeanors* (New York, 1978).

Chapter 3. The Legal Imagination at Work

The transcript: the House Judiciary Committee published a shelf full of documents. The historian who would like to have access to the raw material can consult a twelve-volume set (half of which are themselves multiple books) entitled *Statement of Information* (Washington, D.C., 1974). This set contains the documents assembled by the staff. It is supplemented by four volumes of appendixes, three volumes of testimony of witnesses, four volumes of information submitted on behalf of the president, and a transcript of eight of the tapes. This is a daunting collection, and one may be relieved to know that there is a volume entitled *Summary of Information*; there is also a volume entitled *Report*, which is the final report summarizing the committee's proceeding.

However, in this book I shall allude to none of these items. I am interested not in the documents but in the rhetoric used by the members of the committee in addressing the issues raised by these documents. For my purposes, the key congressional texts are the transcript of the debates, which appear in four volumes; a three-volume set entitled *Impeachment Inquiry* (Washington, D.C.: 1974), which leads up to the final debates; and a volume entitled *Debate on the Articles of Impeachment* (Washington, D.C., 1974), which contains the debates that accompanied the votes on the articles of impeachment. The resolution that is quoted in the text appears in volume 1 of *Impeachment Inquiry* at p. 1; the colloquy between Butler and Doar appears at pp. 5–6 of the same volume.

The Johnson impeachment: I say in the text that the standard history books do not describe it as something to look back upon with pride. For an argument that this customary judgment is incorrect, see Michael Les Benedict, *The Impeachment and Trial of Andrew Johnson* (New York, 1973).

Chapter 4. The Centrally Strategic Charge

The debate on Article III appears in the volume *Debate on Articles of Impeachment*, pp. 449–89. Quotations from it appear as follows: McClory, pp. 451–54; Thornton, p. 455; Wiggins, pp. 458–59; Seiberling, p. 461; Hungate, pp. 484–85; Butler, p. 477; Flowers, p. 483. The text of Article III, as introduced, is at pp. 449–50; the final version is set forth in the Appendix of this book.

Chapter 5. A Crucial Negative Vote

The debate on the tax fraud appears in *Debate on Articles of Impeachment* at pp. 517–60. The passages that I have quoted appear as follows: Mezvinski, pp. 520–22; Waldie, p. 548; Thornton, p. 549.

Chapter 6. Another Negative Vote

The debate on the Cambodia resolution appears in *Debate on Articles of Impeachment* at pp. 489–517. The passages that I have quoted appear as follows: Conyers, pp. 491–92 and, for his opening statement, pp. 37–39; Drinan, pp. 508–10 and, for his opening statement (quoted later in the chapter), pp. 97–99; Cohen, p. 495.

Chapter 7. The Abuse of Power

The debate on the abuse-of-power article occurs in *Debate on Articles of Impeachment* at pp. 333–447. The particular passages quoted appear as follows: Sandman, pp. 423–24; Flowers, p. 405; Edwards, pp. 411–13; McClory, pp. 341–42.

The quotation from Cardozo is taken from the case of *Meinhard* v. *Salmon*, 249 N.Y. 458 (1928).

Chapter 8. Watergate, Narrowly So-Called

The opening statements appear in the volume *Debate on Articles of Impeachment* at pp. 1–136, and the debate on the first article covers pp. 137–331. The passages quoted appear as follows: Rodino, pp. 1–4; Railsback, p. 23; Jordan, pp. 110–13; Hungate, pp. 28–30 and 180–81.

Chapter 9. A Critique

The quotation from Noam Chomsky is taken from his book *Language and Responsibility* (New York, 1979), pp. 20–21.

The John Dean quotation is taken from his book *Blind Ambition* (New York, 1976; Pocket Books, 1977), p. 24.

Chapter 10. Conclusion

The material quoted from James G. Randall's *Constitutional Problems Under Lincoln* (rev. ed., Urbana: University of Illinois Press, 1926) is taken from pp. 514, 513, 519–20, 521–22.

The passage quoted from Caldwell Butler appears in *Debate on Articles of Impeachment* at pp. 68–70. Albert E. Jenner, Jr. was originally minority counsel for the Watergate investigation. However, when John Doar formally recommended impeachment on July 19, 1974, Jenner publicly endorsed this recommendation. The minority members were displeased; they judged his act to be a departure from his appointed role. On July 21, Jenner was ousted as minority counsel and replaced by Samuel A. Garrison III. Jenner remained on the staff and cooperated in the procedure for replacing himself with Garrison. The incident was an expected and understandable by-product of the tensions and pressures of those days (Congressional Quarterly,

Watergate: Chronology of a Crisis, pp. 726–28). For background on the way in which the issue of Jenner's role had been festering among the Republican members, see Fields, *High Crimes and Misdemeanors*, pp. 118–19, 205–6, 215.

Appendix

The official text of the articles of impeachment appears in *Report*, pp. 1–4, 217, 220.

INDEX

Abuse of power: summary of
article, 22; and rule of law, 87–
90, 95–98, 104; procedure, 90–
91; Sandman argues against, 92–
93; Flowers argues for, 94–95;
and democracy, 99–100; Edwards
argues for, 100–102; McClory
argues for, 102–3; and breach of
trust, 104–5

Agnew, Spiro: resigns, 21

Article I. *See* Obstruction of justice

Article II. *See* Abuse of power

Article III. *See* Subpoenas

Article IV. *See* Cambodian bombing

Article V. *See* Tax fraud

Articles of impeachment:
summarized, 22–23; rhetoric of,
38–40

Authority. *See* Legitimacy

Bernstein, Carl, 7

Bork, Robert: fires Cox, 20. *See*
Saturday Night Massacre

Breach of trust: a fundamental
metaphor, 2; theory implied in
articles, 39–40; not debated in
Article V on tax fraud, 72; and
abuse of power, 104–5; in
Rodino's speech, 109–10, 113–
14; and the Saturday Night

Massacre, 132; as a metaphor for
politics, 137–38, 141–42; and
Franklin Delano Roosevelt, 138;
and Abraham Lincoln, 138–41; in
Caldwell Butler's speech, 142–52

Brooks, Jack (member of
committee): voting on articles, 25

Burglars: list of names, 8; indicted,
10; trial, 11–12; sentencing, 14

Burglary, of Democratic National
Committee: date of, 7; political
situation at time of, 8

Burke, Edmund: on prejudices, 3–4,
5; quoted by Rodino, 109, 112

Butler, M. Caldwell (member of
committee): voting on articles,
25; colloquy with Doar on
resolution, 30–33, 35, 66; argues
against Article III, 53–54;
opening statement, 142–52

Butterfield, Alexander: reveals
existence of tapes, 19

Cambodian bombing: summary of
article, 23; summary of
arguments, 75–76; Conyers leads
debates, 77–78; Conyers gives
opening statement on history,
78–80; Drinan argues for, 80–81;
Cohen argues against, 81–82; and

Cambodian bombing (cont'd)
rule of law, 82–83, 86; and
democracy, 82–83, 86; Drinan
interprets constitution, 84–86

Cardozo, Benjamin: on breach of
trust, 105

Character, American: debate
discloses, 1; strange in eyes of
world, 3; and breach of trust,
104–5

Chomsky, Noam: criticizes the
standard praise, 127–28;
overlooks Saturday Night
Massacre, 132

Chotiner, Murray: conversation
with John Dean, 129

Cohen, William S. (member of
committee): voting on articles,
25; argues against Article IV,
81–82

Conyers, John (member of
committee): voting on articles,
25; leads debate on Article IV,
77–80

Cox, Archibald: appointed special
prosecutor, 16; legal proceedings
to get tapes, 19; fired, 20, 132

CREEP (Committee to Re-elect the
President), 9; dirty tricks, 11

Danielson, George E. (member of
committee): voting on articles,
24, 25

Dean, John (counsel to the
president): sits in on FBI
interviews, 13; gives documents
from Hunt's safe to Gray, 13–14;
resigns, 15; asks Sloan to claim
privilege against self-
incrimination, 16; testifies before

Ervin committee, 17, 19; seeks
advice of Murray Chotiner, 129

Democracy: theory of, implied in
articles, 40; vote on Article III
moves away from, 56–57; vote on
Article IV moves away from, 82–
83, 86; Chomsky on, 128–29,
132; and rule of law, 132–33

Dennis, David W. (member of
committee): voting on articles, 25

Doar, John (committee counsel):
leads committee through
evidence, 21; colloquy with
Butler on resolution, 30–33, 35,
66

Donohue, Harold D. (member of
committee): voting on articles,
25; offers resolution, 27–28;
offers Article II, 90; offers Article
I, 107

Drinan, Robert F. (member of
committee): voting on articles,
24, 25; argues in favor of Article
IV, 80–81, 84–86

Edwards, Don (member of
committee): voting on articles,
25; argues for Article II on abuse
of power, 100–102

Ehrlichman, John (chief of domestic
affairs): offers advice on Gray, 14;
resigns, 15; testifies before Ervin
committee, 18

Eilberg, Joshua (member of
committee): voting on articles,
24, 25

Ellsberg, Daniel: Liddy burglary of
psychiatrist's office, 18; status
debated by Sandman, 93; trial,
99–100